Stephan Groborsch

Notes on the Way of St. James

From Bavaria to the Star Field in Spain –> 2500 km on foot!

Herstellung und Verlag: BoD - Books on Demand, Norderstedt
ISBN 978-3-7322-9745-0

Contents

List of snapshots

Credits

Stephan Groborsch	Title picture Sahagun
Stephan Groborsch	figure: 2-4, 6, 9+10, 12-16, 20-22, 26+27, 30-32, 36, 38, 41-44, 46, 48-52, 54-56, 58+59, 62+63, 65-69, 71-73, 76, 78-80, 82, 85, 88, 90, 92, 94-97, 101+102
Diana + Thomas Helgeth	figure: 1, 7+8
Nicole Büchli	figure: 23, 25, 33-35, 40, 45
Google Earth	figure: 61
Wikipedia	figure: 74
Debra	figure: 83+84, 86, 100
Julia Lietz	figure: 103
Garmin	All maps in European MetroGuide v4.00 figure: 5, 11, 17-19, 24, 28+29, 37, 39, 47, 53, 57, 60, 64, 70, 75, 77, 81, 87, 89, 91, 93, 98+99

Conversions

Distances

1 Kilometer = 0.62 US Miles

2500 Kilometer = 1553.424 US Miles

Elevation

1 Meter = 3.28 feet

Temperature

0°C × 1.8 + 32 = 32°F

5°C × 1.8 + 32 = 41°F

20°C x 1.8 + 32 = 68°F

Actors:

Stephan Groborsch	the Pilgrim
Ursula (Uschi) Groborsch	Pilgrim's wife
Diana Helgeth	Pilgrim's daughter
Richard (Richy) Groborsch	Pilgrim's son
Thomas Helgeth	Pilgrim's son-in-law
Reginhard Groborsch	Pilgrim's brother
Klemens Groborsch	Pilgrim's brother
Siegfried Koenig	Pilgrim's brother-in-law
Ivanka Koenig	Pilgrim's sister-in-law
Simone Hauenstein	Daughter of brother-in-law
Gerhard Gulde	Former comrade FBW 34
Monika Blank	Matrone in Lindau
Nicole	Pilgrim from Switzerland
Peter	Pilgrim from Switzerland
Klaus	Pilgrim from Germany
Dietmar	Pilgrim from Germany
Gabriel	Pilgrim from France
Carola Schneck	Catholic parish military aide
Fredy	Pilgrim from Germany
Debra	Pilgrim from USA
Lindsey	Pilgrim from USA
Angelika Mercer	Cousin, translator
Emily Mercer	Cousin's daughter, translator

Introduction

What reasoning could prompt a man to travel 2,500 kilometers by foot? I don't really have a clear answer. When my parents were still alive they often spoke of the Camino de Santiago trail, but I never took it into consideration; life revolved around my wife and children.

So why did I begin walking? Did the trail appeal to me because it was trendy or was it because my brother had already decided I should do it? I'm not sure. I wanted to do something packed with adventure. I wanted an experience, an experience that most people will never have. At that point I was 48 years old. At 49 years old, I informed my wife, family and friends of my intentions. By my 50th birthday the foundations had been laid and everyone knew of my plans, but no one believed I would go!

I prepared myself one step at a time, paying extra attention to studying maps, though I would discover later that my studies didn't always result in success. I still can't properly operate the GPS that I bought for the trip, but that doesn't bother me because I am continuing to learn about this gadget and still use it.

Why am I even writing this down? Perhaps so that one day my grandchildren will read my story, "Grandpa-Adventure!" More importantly, I had to write it down for myself. I experienced so many wonderful moments that I will remember forever. It's very important for me to immortalize my story.

Now, I want to give a few words of thanks.

First and foremost, to my lovely wife for giving me the confidence needed to take on this endeavor. I hope I have made you proud, dear Uschi.

I also want to thank my daughter, who took the time and trouble to read my writing from an editorial view. Her efforts have helped to keep my story alive.

Lastly, I would like to give thanks to the many people I met along the way, for giving me so much joy and acceptance.

Now that the introduction is over, you can enjoy the story.

[signature]

The Pilgrim

Preparations

How did I prepare myself for this adventure? I'd like to write a few sentences on that.

Practical preparation: I tried to buy all the necessary maps with a scale of 1:50,000. For Germany and Switzerland it was no problem. In Germany, French and Spanish maps are difficult to find in this scale. So I reduced the scale to 1:125,000.

The next step was to get a guidebook, which provided plenty of information to plan the route.

The next step was to get a guidebook and plan the route. The guidebooks provided plenty of information to get this done.

A family weekend spent talking about the "Way of St. James", which was organized by the Catholic military priest from Kaufbeuren airbase, was another step in the preparations.

As of October 2010, more and more time went into the planning. My GPS was loaded with maps and routes, which were being constantly refined. At the time I completed my packing list and checked my equipment again and again.

Physical Preparation:

I had to reach a certain level of physical fitness. To that end I put together a little program.

- Monday & Tuesday > running, 8-10km.
- Wednesday > an hour of swimming
- Thursday > running again
- Friday > hiking 15-20 k with at least 10kg in the backpack.

I stayed on this schedule, by and large, until one week before the start.

Day 1, Here we go! Memmingerberg to Herlazhofer Pond

Diana and the children picked me up at 8:00 am, and we took the short cut to the kindergarten.

Figure 1: The first steps

At Fritsch, a house in the neighborhood, we were met by Gulde Gerhard, who gave me money (in the form of a 100 € chocolate coin) to take on my trip. Before the turnoff to the kindergarten, I said goodbye to my grandchildren and Diana. Then I went to Fielmann, an optician, where I gave my wife a big kiss for goodbye.

When I walked through Volkratshofen I went to Stetter, the butcher, but he was closed, unfortunately. What bad luck, I really needed to buy some meat!

The butcher shop in Aichstetten closes on every Wednesday afternoon, but I arrived just in time. I bought some raw pork belly and sausage.

Right now I'm at N47° 57': E10° 03' and attempting to make a fire to cook my lunch. Within half an hour, I have a fire going and meat in the pot! Now I just have to wait for the soup to cook. Lunch was pretty good, and I was able to wash everything in the brook. After that, I strayed from the street, following the forest path instead, where I watched a fox hunt mice until it noticed me and ran off. Later,

I saw a C-160 Transall military carrier practice touch-and-go landings at the Leutkirch airfield. I took my first break near the entrance to the town of Leutkirch. I was tired and I still had to walk about 6 kms, as the crow flies, to get to Herlazhofer Pond.

Figure 2: Preparing lunch

Right now it's another 2 kms to the campsite. I'm tired and anxious to arrive at my destination, but my mood is still good and the weather perfect, though a bit windy. After the break I feel some pain returning, but I hope it will pass! My hip belt has already popped open three times! I have to figure out why this happening.

N47° 46': E10° 00'

I finally arrived at the campsite, owned by the Riedele family, at Herlazhofer Pond. I was in luck; the assistant was off doing repair work, but had left me a camping space, a toilet and beer for seven euros. My dinner was quite enjoyable. I realize now that I must change tomorrow's route because I'm on the wrong side of the pond. It doesn't matter, since there are some good paths to take. Tomorrow I will only go as far as Wangen, so that I don't arrive in Lindau too soon. My pants are already dirty!!!

It is 8 pm now, and I'm sitting at my dining spot. Around 7:55 pm, a Tornado fighter bomber flew overhead at about 300m above ground level, with a wing sweep of 45° and two under-wing tanks. The sound has passed, and now I hear a fairly large bird warbling in the tall pine tree opposite me. It's larger than a blackbird or a thrush, but very pretty. I just finished my second beer, and now the day is over. Unfortunately, I can't send anyone a text message because there is no reception here, so it will have to wait until tomorrow.

Now it's time to kick-back for the night. I will probably go to bed at 10:30 CEST (Central European Summer Time).

Figure 3: First camp at Herlazhofer pond

Daily kms	Total kms
33.9	33.93

Day 2, Herlazhofer Pond to Wangen

The night was ok. The tent is a little snug, but I'll get used to it. I was awakened by a light rain. It's time to wear the Goretex and put the rain cover over my backpack. I'll find reasonably cheap lodging in Wangen. Maybe an inexpensive hostel or monastery? So far I haven't read any spiritual text, so let's see how this goes. It's now 6:30 am, and it will probably take me until 8am to get everything gathered together.

Uschi has to do inventory today! Oh poor lady, I am thinking of you!

First stop: It's raining lightly, and there are frequent breaks in the rain — no problem! I can already see that the weather is beautiful to the southwest. In 50 meters, I'll be back on the planned path. I've crossed the lower Argen valley! I had to remove the Goretex; the sun is shining and I've become extremely warm. The wind is pleasant and refreshing.

I've arrived at Ratzenried: lunch - a beer, pork belly sandwich, and an apple.

Wangen: I asked about accommodations at the tourist bureau, and was referred to the Baumgarten Inn. Single occupancy with breakfast for 25 euros, but breakfast didn't start till 8am.

Summary of this day: a deviation from the campground has caused me to change the intended path from Ratzenried to Wangen. I meant to follow the directions, yet found myself in the hill country. The view was superb, but the constant ups and downs! I suspect I'm drinking too little, my urine is too yellow and my calves are cramping. Klemens sent me a nice text message - it's as if he's on the trail with me! Yikes, I'm having chafing issues! I probably need to moisturize more often. Today I'll have access to warm water! Hurray!

Daily kms	Total kms
20.9	55.03

Day 3, The First Pilgrim in Lindau: Wangen to Lindau

I had a quiet night at the inn. In the bar yesterday, I solved a Sudoku puzzle and read the newspaper, all the while observing the other guests: a group at a table enjoying a healthy round of "Schafkopf" (a popular card game in Southern Germany), the landlady speaking with some regular patrons about world events, and at the fourth table two couples were eating dinner. One woman talked constantly about her job at the hospital, while the other three just listened. Today I won't be able to leave before 8:30 am, because breakfast isn't served until 8:00 am. It would have been nice to leave at 7:30 am and already be on the path. Also, I began reading the New Testament yesterday (before the beer). We'll see how far I get.

First break: Untermoorweiler: So far, the "bike path 1" has been very hilly. My calf muscles no longer hurt, probably because the lactic acid is gone. The weather is optimal with a thin layer of clouds, I'm in a great mood and sometimes I think about the New Testament. What did I read yesterday and did I really understand all of it?

Midday: I haven't found a butcher shop along the way. Lunch will be onion soup with carrots, garlic and nettle. This time I got the fire started even faster, and without the Esbit stove - fantastic!

I'm now in the Pilgrim's hostel in Lindau. A woman opened the door and was totally surprised! I called her three times but she had left her cell phone at home. After a moment of shock (about five minutes) she let me in. Sunday, 4/3/2011, is the grand opening with the mayor and some others. This is her, Monika, and she is very excited and doing basic cleaning! She pulled herself together, and we drank coffee while my clothes were in the wash.

Figure 4: The first pilgrim in Lindau with Monika

She gave me a few tips and suggestions for my trip. In the evening, I went to dinner and then to bed early.

Daily kms   Total kms

20.4   75.65

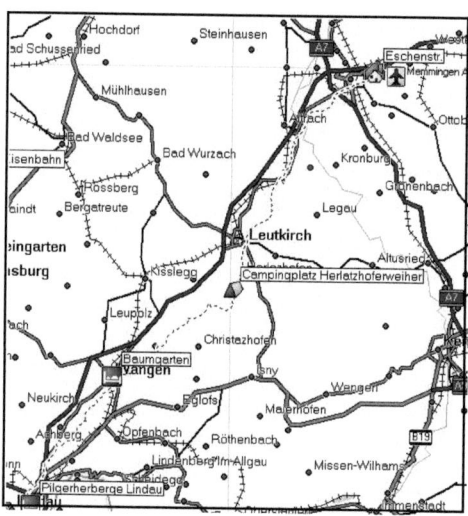

Figure 5: Trail > Memmingerberg - Lindau

Day 4, Lindau to St. Gallen

I slept well at the Pilgrim's Hostel. I paid 8 euros for my accommodations and 4.99 euros for new batteries for the GPS. The grilled onion soup and drinks I had yesterday totaled 22 euros. I encountered Monika again on my way back. She seems like a happy woman. She's still concerned because I am alone, so she gave me her home phone number. Nice. Diana called yesterday, and we've arranged to meet on the island of Lindau at around noon. Now it's time to eat breakfast and get ready. Monika came by again to give me her blessing and a photo of me in front of the hostel.

Figure 6: In front of the hostel in Lindau

First break: In the harbor I had a huge shock. The captain of the ferry who docked said there won't be another connection to Rorschach until April 17th. After a long conversation and the help of another man, we found a solution: the Swiss are sailing! Now I'm waiting at the harbor for Diana and her family, having quickly eaten two meatballs. I'm a bit nervous about the footpath to St. Gallen, but my backpack is comfortable and my calves feel fine.

Figure 7: My daughter, Diana and her children

Figure 8: Here with my son-in-law Thomas

At 1:15 pm I'm sitting on the sun deck of the Rynegg, heading toward Rorschach. The Helgeth family is standing on the wharf, waving until the ship leaves the harbor. Splendid!!!

23

From Rorshach to my next stop is an hour and forty minute hike uphill. I'll take a break. The average speed that my GPS shows isn't correct (my GPS tracks everything), because I took a ship across Lake Constance.

The Martinsbrugg, a bridge that spans a deep ravine that was carved by the Goldach River, is a critical spot for me. Before the bridge existed, early pilgrims had to walk down into the ravine and back up to cross, a very dangerous undertaking.

Brilliant sunshine! I reached the Pilgrim's Hostel on the phone. They said I was an hour away from the hostel (20 SFr)! But that hour turned into an hour and a half. For a while I thought I had already passed it, but with patience and my cell phone I finally got there.

So far the hike has been exhausting, though always rewards me with beautiful views. It was so wonderful that Diana and her family came to Lindau.

At the Pilgrim's Hostel, I was welcomed by two sisters (siblings, not nuns), and another man. I learned that his name is Goetz, and he is from Lausanne. He began this morning in Rorschach, and is making a pilgrimage home. He has some excellent maps that he found on the internet at www.suisse.@mobile.ch. Yikes, it's already 9:30 pm and I've just now finished dinner. I purchased a few things from the train station earlier. Tomorrow is Saturday! I don't know yet how far I will travel, but I should probably put sunscreen on more often. I am sunburnt on both arms! Now it's time to stop!!!

Daily kms	Total kms
35.7	111.31

Day 5, St. Gallen to Wald

Today is Sunday, and Goetz and I are having a conversation about God and the world. We simply can't get going. I still need to wash-up, brush my teeth, etc. It was 9:30am when I finally marched out of the hostel. I found the road to Herisau by following the various path markers, which are well marked with a shell symbol.

First break: I saw many Swiss cycling or taking a leisurely walk; most of them are friendly. I almost missed an important turn, but a friendly woman showed me the right way! What does it say in Matthew in the New Testament: "Don't worry ..." I ate lunch on a bench overlooking Herisau, with a view, a fire pit, and wind—so beautiful!

Figure 9: Viewpoint of Herisau

Fixing lunch is increasingly faster and easier. Tomorrow I will buy two each of potatoes, carrots, onions, and cook them with some pork belly—delicious!

Afternoon break: the path is strenuous with the altitude changing constantly. The fountains have all been shut off and I will need fresh water soon! I still don't know where today's stopping point will be! About the water, look to Matthew: Don't worry ...""! A boy brought me some water from his house because the fountains "have some unhealthy bacteria in the water!" In upper Wittenberg, I consulted my navigation tools and maps and decided to stay at a campground in the village of Wald. Hopefully it's open!

Figure 10: Tent in Wald

I arrived at the Wald campground, which is an ideal place to pitch a tent. The site's owner set up an extra table and chair for me, so now I can eat and write in my journal more comfortably. I'm not sure yet how far I will travel tomorrow! I was fortunate to be able to speak with the site's owner. She's an open-minded woman in her early 90's (I'm guessing). We had a riveting conversation about past and present politics. It is so poignant to speak with someone who lived through those times. She told me about her experiences during World War II, and the relationship between the leading powers on both sides. She also explained to me how the scattered settlements of the Appenzell region came to be. "Long ago, a giant from Austria was carrying a sack across his shoulders that was filled with farmhouses. His intent was to drop them along Lake Zurich in Switzerland, but the sack had a hole in it, and so, little by little, the houses fell to the Earth in Appenzell. When the giant arrived at the lake, the sack was empty. And as he looked around, he saw that everything was alright and so he left them where they remain to this day." A clue to the poor relationship between Austria and Switzerland can be found in this story. The site owner herself, however, has a good relationship with her Austrian neighbors. Then the conversation was interrupted by her husband, who wanted his dinner.

Daily kms	Total kms
16.7	128.19

Day 6, Wald to Rapperswil

I was awakened by rain at 5:30 this morning. I quickly moved the tent and the rest of my equipment to the shower's entryway to dry out. Rain! It has ruined my mood today. Yesterday I had a couple beers in a local pub (15 SFr) while charging my cell phone. I talked with some people there who said that my plan is really great, though I still feel that I'm just starting out. The night at the campground cost 11 SFr.

The rain has gotten heavier and the path to Rapperswil is far! I have decided to take the road, because the Way of St. James passes through forests and over meadows, and I'm afraid I'll slip and fall. Next I must get to Wattwil. In Peterzell I acquired lodging for 13 SFr.

First break: Wasserfluh Pass. I only ate an apple, because the rain is so shitty. On the way down to Wattwil I experienced some digestive troubles. The mixture of calcium, magnesium, and a multi-vitamin must be too much. I'd better leave out the magnesium! In Wattwil/Bunt I hurried into a Shell gas station. The attendant looked at me, dressed in Goretex with a look of desperation on my face, as if I had come from another planet, but the toilet was mine!!!!!

Midday: I'm continuing on the bike path to Ricken. After that is still undecided. Lunch was not very good because I didn't have a sufficient amount of Esbit fuel. Now I need to orient myself toward Rapperswil. I'll walk about 10-15 kms, then take a bus.

Afternoon Break: From here it's still 20 km to Rapperswil. I walked to the nearest bus stop, where I don't have to wait very long for the next bus. I'm completely soaked. The Goretex isn't drying very well! I contacted the Pilgrim's Hostel and reserved a spot.

I'm in the hostel in Rapperswil, very classy. There are five pilgrims today. For the first time, I am not alone: two women (in their 60's) from Switzerland, a "pro-pilgrim" and her sister, a novice pilgrim. Then a young married man who was given four months of vacation time to complete a pilgrimage to Rome. The young man (about 30) and I ate pizza and had a nice conversation.

I didn't drink any beer today, but I did have a glass of red wine. The day has been miserable. It rained the entire time, and I had to walk along the road. I did not take the original route for the Way of St. James because it led over grassy hills in the Alpenzeller region. I had concerns about slipping and being forced to stop. The little scam is that I've ridden the bus about 19 kms. I don't think it will make much of a difference, however. Tomorrow I'm going to Einsiedeln, which also has a Pilgrim's Hostel. The altitude will be increasing sharply.

Daily kms	Total kms
45	173,25

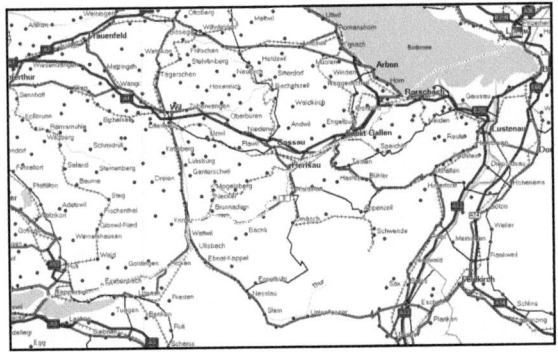

Figure 11: Trail > Lindau - Rapperswil

Day 7 Rapperswil to Trachselau

Expenses from yesterday: rations 13.00 SFR, bus 4.50 SFR, hostel 20.00 SFR, pizza 34.00 SFR.

I'm going to get rid of my rain fly and the poles for it. The rain fly is too small to fit over the tent, and the Goretex has been more useful for waterproofing. The main problem with rain is that when I'm walking into it, it gets my face wet and drips down onto my chest. And when the indoor and outdoor temperatures are almost the same, the Goretex doesn't allow sweat to evaporate. Yesterday I feared that I was getting a cold, but my fear proved to be unfounded. So, how far will I travel today? Einsiedeln or Alptal?

First break: The altitude jumped from 407 meters to 536 meters in about 55 minutes! Super sunshine! In Rapperswil I ditched my rain fly and its poles and sent mail to Diana.

Figure 12: View of Lake Zurich with Rapperswil in the background.

Midday break: I built a fire at Hixenstein. The view opens over the plateau of Einsiedeln. Particularly impressive is the view of the Great Mythen! It makes you feel so tiny! Gigantic is too small a word to describe it. The first feelings of happiness come over me. On the left, in the foreground, is the Sihl Sea with the snow-covered Alps in the background. Here too, gigantic is insufficient to describe the scene.

Einsiedeln monastery: I briefly looked around the church, prayed, and then paused to make some decisions about the day's destination. Trachselau is within range. Then I'll be closer to the Haggenegg. I have lodging at a bed and breakfast in Trachselau for 30 SFR. I ate dinner in the room, showered, and then went out for a beer at the town's only restaurant.

I had an idea along the way; I wanted to remember it, but I forgot. Next time I'll pause right away to write down my thoughts.

Daily kms   Total kms

17.2   191.24

Figure 13: A pilgrim in front of the Einsiedeln

Day 8, Trachselau to Ingenbohl

It was a peaceful night. It's cloudy today, but there's no precipitation. I got my traveler's stamp in the church of Trachselau. I heard from Bohner, my niece, that fog has stranded people in Halong Bay. Hopefully it will pass soon, and everything will be lovely again.

A word about yesterday: The view of the two Mythen Mountains on the way to Einsiedeln sparked deep feelings in me which, for the first time, I could feel in my cheeks. It's 7:30am and I'm waiting for breakfast, then immediately after I'll be on my way again.

First stop: I'm at the Haggenegg, but the pub doesn't open until May 1st! Oh well, I can go without beer, although I'd have really liked to eat a sausage. I expected snow at the summit but there was sunshine, and I had to walk through only 2 meters of 10cm deep snow. I have eaten the last of the power bars Klemens gave me. Along the way, I find myself thinking about Uschi, Diana and her family, especially the two youngest, Jaron and the unborn baby. God has been good to me, the weather is perfect. Important: The GPS' reception is invalid when it's on a metal table. To clarify - the GPS shows false data. As I watched the compass on the GPS, it pointed in the wrong direction for north. When I took the device off the metal tabletop, it pointed in the correct direction again!

Figure 14: At Haggenegg

Midday: The potatoes were much better this time! The sisters from Rapperswil have passed me during lunch. I stir my soup while my shirt and undershirt are drying.

Figure 15: View over Lake of Vierwaldstetter and Schwyz

I've arrived at the Ingenbohl monastery! I have a four-person room all to myself (B&B 31.25 SFR, of which tax is 1.25 SFr). Sister Irene gave me some suggestionsof things to do in the monastery. I attended vespers, then morning prayers and mass the next day. The ship to Beckenried doesn't leave until tomorrow morning at 9:49 am, so I've got plenty of time. Unfortunately, I could not do my laundry at the monastery. I bought groceries at Migros, and now have ingredients for two meals. I ended the day with a smoked sausage and a beer; my world is now in order.

Tomorrow I'm traveling from Brunnen to Beckenried by boat, because I hate the idea of walking unnecessary elevations. Sister Irene will make breakfast tomorrow morning, and following communion I'll be ready to go.

Figure 16: The Mountains from Ingenbohl and the Haggenegg.

Daily kms   Total kms

15.9   207.63

Figure 17: Trail > Rapperswil - Ingenbohl monastery

Day 9, Ingenbohl to Bethanien

6:45 found me at morning prayers followed by attendance at the morning Mass. Sister Irene is currently on pilgrim duty, so she made breakfast and gave me an apple for the road. How stupid that I bought two apples for the road yesterday. I got a text from Diana—she doesn't know where Einsiedeln is! I need to contact Klemens about lodging in Kerns. Maybe I can do that before I actually get there. My niece, Simi, gave me a call. I have declared Holy Week as my arrival time in Geneva. I also talked to her mother, Ivanka; short conversations aren't possible! I took a boat to Beckenried and found the first path markers. Now I'm off.

Midday and the first break: I won't be cooking until later today or tomorrow. I need to decide how far I'll travel today. St Nicholas would be nice! Crap, not all the routes are loaded into the GPS. There are no routes beginning with the letters N-Z. Okay then, I'll navigate myself and follow the signs.

Second break: Having a beer. I should be in St. Nicholas by 4:00pm. I've been distracted by the air traffic at Strans. I'm moving on now—ready, set, go!

I've reached the St. Nicholas monastery, Bethany House: my room is 50 SFr (room and a meal). I arrived at the monastery at 6:25 pm and was quickly shown to my room because dinner was served at 6:30 pm. Usually I unpack my gear first, but today I had to quickly shower and then get down to dinner. Also at the table was a priest, who is staying here in return for saying the daily Mass. A pleasant conversation. Dinner was fantastic; a three-course menu consisting of a meat soup with vegetables, generous portions of ham and cheese toast and salad, and cottage cheese with apples for dessert. After dinner I washed my clothes, rinsed some dishes, and sorted my gear. Now I can reflect back on the day and make plans for tomorrow. While following the path from Beckenried, I was unsure about my goals for the day. I didn't want to power walk, but as I've stated before, the sound of aircraft engines constantly pull me into their spell—pity! For this time of year, it is unseasonably hot in Nidwalden and Obwalden. I had expected cooler weather. Even though they got plenty of snow, the farmers complained because it melted too quickly and now it won't rain. I've disturbed the first lizards in their sunbathing. It probably won't rain in the next few days, and I can manage on 6 liters of water. So now I should give some thought to tomorrow's route. Tomorrow's plan, Bruenningpass - no! In Obsee or in Lungern looking for cheap lodging - yes! Important: I heard from my sweetheart today! And I also called my in-laws, Sigi and Ivanka.

Daily kms	Total kms
34.6	242.2

Day 10, Bethanien to Lungern

First break: The hike has been great so far. I temporarily lost the Way of St. James, but continued following the lake. I found only one fire pit, but the people of Obwalden are very neat and had cleared away all the old wood, so I'll be having a cold lunch again.

Second break: Some things (like a restroom) cannot be delayed. Thank God I was approaching a town. Since beginning the pilgrimage, my rate of digestion has increased rapidly. I should probably only add one mineral tablet to my canteen. Problem solved, so I reward myself with a beer! Earlier this morning, after Mass, we enjoyed a pleasant breakfast. My dining partner was also the celebrant of the mass, and we had a short, lively conversation. Since I was an early-in-the-year pilgrim, the nuns and staff gave me a lavish sendoff. Oh, and I also learned about the hermitage of Brother Klaus, who was instrumental in connecting the areas of Nidwalden and Obwalden to Switzerland, on the Flueli-Rampf. So now I'm finishing my beer, then I'm off again.

I've arrived at the Lungern campsite. There are washers and dryers! The tent has been set up. Now all I need is some money and dinner.

Daily kms	Total kms
17.1	259.36

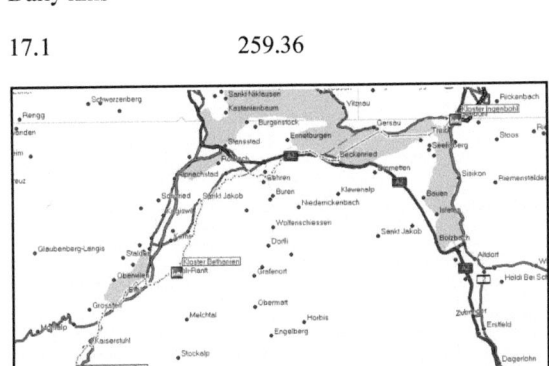

Figure 18: Trail > Ingenbohl monastery - Lungenersee

Day 11, Lungern to Ringgenberg

After a pleasant night and meager breakfast, I approached the Brunning Pass. It was exhausting, though the elevation didn't rise much. Yesterday I wanted to get a little something to eat, some money, and some postcards to write. That little something turned out to be a horse meat steak. Yum! Yum! In the pub at the campground I drank "ne Stange" (the Swiss name for a 1/3 liter of beer), looked over Sudoku, and read the weather forecast. Monika from Lindau sent me her email address.

First break: I have conquered the Brunning Pass and am in Brienzweiler. I sent Diana a letter and drank a beer. The descent was slow-going; the unevenness of the path was difficult to see because it was hidden by the fallen leaves of beech trees. I walked very carefully to prevent twisting my right foot. Yes, my right ankle sometimes buckles and then I have to relax it until the tendons have settled down. The leaves were ankle high in some areas, thank God it was dry!

Second break: the GPS has a mind of its own—the data isn't plausible. It automatically turned itself off. I expect a continuation of these errors and will recalculate and evaluate it when I get home. Another cold lunch today! These orderly Swiss! The ferry service is still closed for winter, so I guess I'll have to walk. We'll see how far it is to Lake Thun.

Third break: Searching for accommodations. It probably won't be easy to find one here at the lake! Campsite! I've set up my tent and showered with a semblance of warm water for 1.00 SFr. I've done almost everything right in the shower. Tossed my money in and got into shower stall two, which must have been the wrong shower! I realized my error after I finished showering. The other shower had hot water—oops! So now it's clear, the GPS has data failures totaling 5.5 kms—>279.99 kms. I'd better keep an eye on my GPS tomorrow. Now and then today it has made life miserable. Add to that the loneliness I felt while setting up my tent.

Daily kms	Total kms
15.6	274.99

Day 11, Ringgenberg to Hilterfingen

I slept well in the tent last night. I wasn't cold at all, even though the mat is defective. I need to find tape somewhere to repair it. I am sitting at breakfast in Interlaken, and the chestnut trees are obstructing my view of the Eiger, Moench and Jungfrau mountains. Yesterday I had a bratwurst, and am now enjoying a delicious braided bread just the way my sweetheart and I like it—by pulling it apart piece by piece. Now life is flowing back into me!

Second break by the St. Beatus Caves! I am content.

Third break and lunch, in Merlingen now. I've encountered plentiful hills and dales along nice forest paths and also the street. I'll eat a little so I get energy for the rest of the day.

Short break: confirmed quarters in Hilterfingen! Super! Now I need to load a new section of maps! *grins*

I've arrived at the "Neb-Thun Lodge" in Hilterfingen on Lake Thun! A nice room but no dryer, unfortunately. But the sun is shining directly on the balcony, so I think the clothes will dry. Tomorrow I will reach Thun and, hopefully, pass it. We'll see how far I get. The route along the lake was extremely hilly but, in the end, much more comfortable than the asphalt, like yesterday. For dinner I had the worst pizza in Switzerland and the ambiance was a bit pretentious. Uschi seems to be doing well, so I'll read for a little while.

Daily kms   Total kms

21.6   296.72

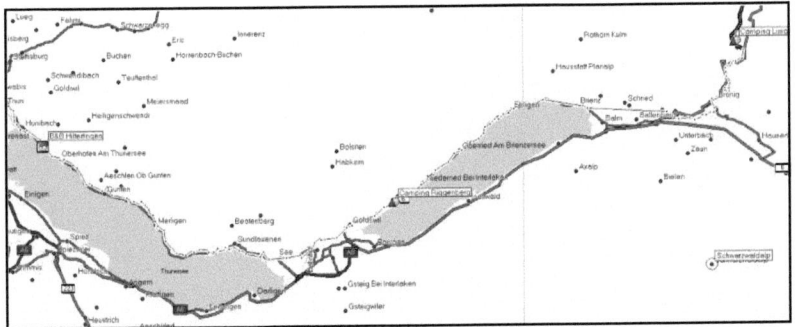

Figure 19: Trail > Lungenersee - Hilterfingen

Day 12, Hilterfingen to Muribogen

I slept very well and will be happy if I manage to get to Wattenwil! I have to get money again in Thun; the weekend was expensive, even though I spent two nights in my tent. My rations planning was lousy. Saturday and Sunday took me by surprise —> sloppy!

First break: Allmendingen; went shopping! Woo Hoo! I got some eggs and a drink, plus money in Thun.

Second break: Making lunch with the rest of the Esbit fuel. I received a text message from Siegfried with the weather forecast for the next few days. Today is still good, but starting tomorrow it will be much cooler with some precipitation. Now my cell phone is doing what it wants! It wants to navigate! It drains the battery and eats up data from the network. Thomas' Christmas gift, a portable solar-powered charger for the cell phone, works.

Figure 20: A bed in a haystack

The bed and breakfast in Riggisberg has no vacancies, so I phoned "Sleeping on Straw". Success! Accommodations reserved! An hour's walk and another 60m of altitude gained. Result —>a huge straw billet all to myself (alas, where is Uschi?).

Figure 21: Here I relaxed my feet (barefoot way)

The farmer's wife told me all that I needed to know, and even persuaded me to try her barefoot path. So after a quick shower and change, I was ready for the barefoot adventure. It felt strange after a long hike. A warm foot-bath with seasonal flowers followed.

That was so satisfying. When my feet relaxed and the water cooled off, I dried myself. Then to finish my foot care I massaged on some original "Muribogen Calendula Ointment." And what is written in Matthew: Don't worry ... This way of thinking enters my mind often. I found it idiotic at first, but it has now made me content on my path.

Daily kms   Total kms

26.5   323.24

Day 13, Muribogen to Freiburg

I was well rested after a night in the straw and served a hearty breakfast of homemade cheese, homemade strawberry jam and raspberry yogurt (homemade, of course!) The road to Schwarzenburg was pleasant, and the rain that was forecast was just a shower and not at all annoying. The GPS has turned itself off again! I don't know why!

First break: Schwarzenburg; in the pub because of the wind and needing a bathroom.

Second break: I've arrived in Tafers sooner than expected. It appears that Freiburg is only an hour away. I'm hoping to stay on schedule because my pants need to be either mended or thrown out. I'd prefer the former, so that I can wear them until I get to Geneva. In Tafers I saw the "chicken miracel" (I'll get to this later). The weather is okay; better than I imagined.

I've arrived in Freiburg! The path led me to the lowest point in Freiburg and then finally back up the mountain. Phew, I have found the youth hostel!

I'm sharing an 8-bed room with some young French speaking guys. The last time I removed my rain gear, my pants made an audible tear. I went to Migros to buy a needle and thread. I'll probably need to sew them today. The jeans should hold up until I get to Geneva, that is, at least three more days.

I must contact Simi, who lives in Geneva, before making further plans. I'll have to wait until tomorrow because I can't reach her.

Daily kms   Total kms

23.4   346.71

Day 14, Freiburg to Romont

First break: Posieux; I mended my pants last night after dinner. They're holding up pretty well, and as I've said, I hope they last another 3 or 4 days. Sleeping in the straw was more comfortable than last night if only because of the fresh air, unlike that 8-bed room at the hostel that felt like being in an animal cage. I'm expecting troubles today! I don't have a reason to think this, except that I have felt something in my heel for the last four days. Enough moaning, let's go!

Second break: Lunch in Autigny; question is, can I find enough wood to get a fire going and cook? I'll try. It's an old firepit! Surprisingly it burns like tinder and my soup is cooking after only 15 minutes! Today the potatoes and carrots will be tender! The meal was good. The creek was helpful for putting out the fire and washing dishes. Ok.

Figure 22: First time the soup is well done

Apple break: Romont is in sight, about four kilometers away! I'll say it again, I did it! Phew, now an apple, and then I'll go on.

Goal achieved, Romont: I'm staying at a bed and breakfast overlooking the Grand Rue of Romont! It's pretty chaotic in the house—the woman has one child of her own and three other children in her daycare. The living room is organized chaos, but in the guest quarters everything is in tip-top shape. The building is very old. I took a bath and didn't feel guilty, even though the place is inexpensive and the innkeeper is doing my laundry. The clothes are being washed and even the pajamas got thrown in because, as I've been meaning to write down, while on this journey I wake up between 11pm and 1:30am drenched in sweat. I don't dream and otherwise feel fine. I don't know where this comes from. After I turn over two or three times I fall asleep again. So far it's been every night. Strange. After shopping today I ate dinner in my room! It was as good as today's lunch, so I don't think I'll send the cookware home. As for the seam on the pants I fixed yesterday, they passed the first test on the road. We'll see how they fare in the washing machine. So, enough for today I still need to glue foil for my map pocket, prepare tomorrow's route and also read a bit!

Figure 23: Romont

Daily kms	Total kms
22.3	368.97

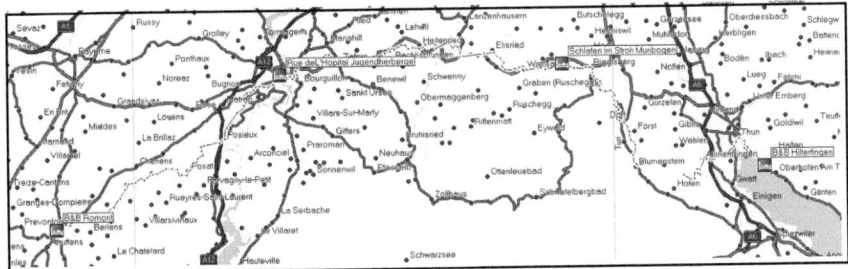

Figure 24: Trail > Hilterfingen - Romont

Day 15, Romont to Chalet-a-Gobet

First break: On the path from Romont to Moudon, about 5 kms from Moudon. I had a nice breakfast of saffron rolls with butter and a spread made from ground mustard seeds, cinnamon and pear juice. It's not for everyone. On my way to a transmission tower I noticed an aircraft formation: an Einmot Turboprop escorted by an F-16 Fighting Falcon and covered by another F-16 in 6 o'clock position, heading for Geneva airport, I suspect. I think I'm leaving Moudon, but I'm not certain. Simi hasn't answered the text I sent her. I'll try calling her during my next break.

Midday in Moudon: ate a sandwich and drank a beer.

Third break: The north wind is pushing me toward the south. There are no beds avaiable, so I'll catch the next bus, which leaves at 5:26 pm.

So now I'm sitting in a bus for the second time in Switzerland, unfortunately, but it's too far to walk the 2 1/2 hours to the next possible lodging. After 33.1 kms, I got off the bus and entered the campground, only half of which was open. I traveled 33.1 - 24.4 = 8.7kms that I rode on the bus. The tent is set up. When I paid for my site, I got 2.00 SFR back because I'm a pilgrim. So 18.00 SFr instead of 20.00 SFr. Now to plan for tomorrow.

While I was sitting and planning the next day I looked at my phone. I was really irritated at it! Once again, it is searching maps and wants to navigate. It drains the power endlessly, so I've got to find a way to stop this. Ugh!

Daily kms	Total kms
34	402.99

Day 16, Chalet-a-Gobet to Rolle

Metro service: 78% humidity - 1012 HPs - 873 meters above sea level - 0 Celsius (32 F).

The night was okay. I slept well, having only woken once due to wind and a blister. And by the way, my phone is fully charged. While dismantling the tent I discovered ice on the outer side of the fabric and realized why my fingers felt stiff. It's now ten after seven; maybe I can get a hot cup of coffee for breakfast here before I go on my way. By the way, yesterday I repaired my insulated mat and it's holding up well.

Figure 25: A look at the roofs of Lausanne

I arrived at Port Ouchy after 2 1/2 hours of downhill mountains, 90% of which was on a busy asphalt road! Now I need to familiarize myself with the official route, which I wandered from about an hour ago. It wasn't bad, the way turned downhill toward the southwest. At the harbor I went into a bar. 1/3 liter of beer was quite expensive at 8.00SFR. Today's target is St. Prex, since Simi isn't home on Monday. I'm walking slowly and enjoying the area.

Oh, my poor son, Richy! He is taking care of my garden. He called to say he is struggling with the lawn mower while I've crossed the 400km line.

I've reached St. Prex! The hotel ad in Outdoor (a tour book) no longer exists. I asked about hotels at the Tourism Bureau, but no one wants any pilgrims. Alternative camping ... again! I happened upon a Swiss supplier who agreed to give me a ride to a campground in Rolle. 33.9 - 24.1 = 9.8 km of riding again. My plan to slowly wander toward Geneva by Tuesday has been thrown out. A B&B in the next town had no vacancies, which tells me that there are more pilgrims on the road than I thought. There was no choice, so I went to the campground. If I followed the pilgrim guide I would've been at Simi's on Monday, but she's busy out of town. That means I should arrive Tuesday afternoon at the earliest. So now a new plan!

Daily kms	Total kms
33.9	437.04

Figure 26: Last time in tent

41

Day 17, Rolle to Gland

The night was okay. I even stayed in bed till 7am, though I've left time to break camp. I'm drinking coffee that cost 4 SFR and then I'll go on to Gland, where there will be a pilgrim hostel.

As I've said, I have time until Tuesday. What should I do with the tent? Carry it to Lourdes? I think that'd be advantageous, judging by the last few days. Or should I say "Do not worry ..." I'm standing in front of the hostel, but don't enter because of my lack of French language skills.

Figure 27: A typical breakfast while camping in Switzerland

So now it's 2pm and everything (almost everything) is done. The washing machine needs another 1 1/2 hours. I've got money in my wallet and went shopping at Denner. I've been admitted to the hostel, which is simple and very clean! Denner a grocery store was out of pork, so I had to find something else appropriate. Yes, two slices leg of veal. I then cooked it in the kitchen, making a delicious soup a la Stephan the Pilgrim. Everything was tender. But first, a tomato salad just the way I like it, with lots of onion and olive oil. Clean up is done, so now I'm lying in front of the hostel, reading in the sunlight. Good thing I brought my swim trunks. On my way here, I met a pilgrim returning home! He started in the area of Le Puy and wanted to reach Rolle to catch the train to his home, which is near my hometown. I think he made it and will be home around 11pm. He advised me to leave the tent in Geneva. Now it is time to lay down in the backyard for some sun, take a nap and enjoy myself.

Daily kms	Total kms
10.9	447.95

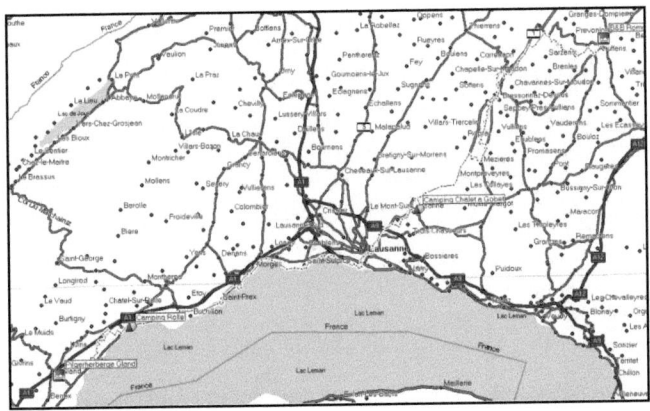

Figure 28: Trail > Romont - Gland

Day 18, Gland to Commugny

First break: I took a brief break to gather my thoughts.

I left for Gland after a good breakfast (I went shopping yesterday) and bad coffee (first instant coffee in years). I got rid of it. I feel that Tuesday's schedule with Simi is a little strange. The accommodations problem from Sunday to Monday is pushing me toward Geneva. Silly! I'm glad to be alone on this journey so that I don't have to take anyone else into consideration. Having only myself to look after makes me feel free! I want to get to France! Here, above Lake Geneva, you see either industry or luxury housing and asphalt.

Second break: Sitting in the Founex village square and no pub in this town! Where do these folks meet up? No toast, so I'll have a power bar; I can shop again tomorrow. Incidentally, the blister on the little toe of my right foot has simply disappeared. It's about 2.5-3 kms to Commugny, let's see if I can find a bed and breakfast there. Wow, I'm in luck. The hotel I thought was closed gave me a room with a shower and toilet, but no lunch. Thank God there's a nearby pub that's open on Sundays. Here I have wine (white) and spaghetti Bolognese. Simi originally thought that Monday she would be on work trip and wouldn't get back home until midnight. How does that work with children? No idea! Last night, Saturday, I called her around 9 pm and asked if I still could come on Monday. It turns out she's not taking a work trip after all, the kids are sick! I need to slow down and stay one more night in Switzerland. As of now, accommodations are expensive. Too bad! Time-wise I'm on schedule. Sitting around isn't very much fun.

Daily kms	Total kms
15.8	463.79

Day 19 Commugny to Geneva

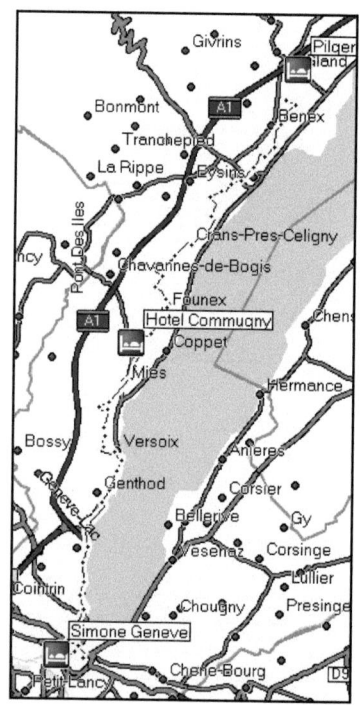

Figure 29: Trail > Gland - Geneva

I have to put in another slow day, because Simi needs her time, so I ate breakfast late. My wife is probably already sitting on the plane home from vacation in Frankfurt. Let's see what the day brings for me.

First break: Versoix, a very nice trail that I really enjoyed. I also enjoyed the view to the other side of Lake Geneva.

Second break: I'll call Simi and go to her house today! She gave me some instructions, because she won't be home until late.

Arrived at Simi's flat: I'll change clothes and go into town, I've got time. Simi has organized everything wonderfully! Her father-in-law moved the backpack into the flat while I was in the city. After my city tour, I reviewed my pack's contents and realized I don't have another pair of hiking pants, but everything else is accounted for, as expected. I had no way of knowing that I would lose weight and my pants wouldn't fit anymore. I've repacked the equipment and the travel guide as well all the maps I need in France. The Swiss papers I left with Simi and I'll get them when I return home. I spent the rest of the day hanging around Geneva. Well, now my pants have to last until Le Puy. My Sweet, I've arrived a day early in Geneva. It's late, though I've made myself comfortable in Vanja's (Simi's first daughter) room on my insulated mat in my sleeping bag. I'm looking forward to France even though the description is not as alluring as it once was and costs will, undoubtedly, rise. Oh Well!

Daily kms   Total kms

15.2   479.01

Day 20, Arrived in France; Geneva to Beaumont

First break: Breakfast and parting from Simi were cordial. She had a lot of plans for me! It turns out I did her an injustice. She and her husband had everything beautifully organized. That's what comes from forming judgments about a person or thing. I said thank you for bed & breakfast and good bye.

I went to the church and looked for the stamp. I didn't find the stamp for my pilgrim pass at the specified location (outdoor, tour guide), doesn't matter. I heard from Bohner that my wife and Alfi (a friend) are sitting on a train on their way back home.

Figure 30: First break in France.

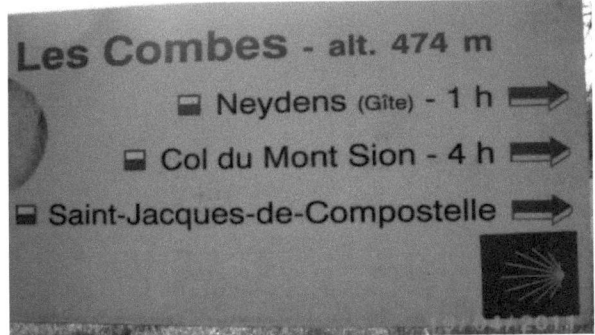

Figure 31: Sometimes it's not worth the time to formulate a goal.

Figure 32: Motivational sign.

Second Break: Midday, I have to save space for my notes written on the backs of maps. Today's menu is chicken strips with potatoes and salad. This was the first really good place on the French side.

I've arrived at the first gîte (hostel)! Okay, I have to get used to the fact that obtaining to shelter will be easier now. An Australian couple and a young Swiss woman are here, too. We're having a wonderful time. And the pants get another chance— I'm sitting here with needle and thread making every effort to save them for as long as possible.

Figure 33: First Gîte from the outside & the inside.

Daily kms   Total kms

17.5   496.51

Day 21, Beaumont to Chaumont

First break: I had a really entertaining time with the Australian couple yesterday (she's 70, he's 72). The night was okay, except for a few bees! On the upper beds, where I slept, was an alternate entrance to a bee nest! I just realized it during the night when I got stung three times. The road, so far, is pleasant but very hilly! This is probably because I lost my way and dragged the Australians along. How nice that I saw incredibly beautiful ancient beech trees.

Figure 34: Just a break

Second break: Lunch: I found a fire pit and am good to go. My pilgrim soup was tasty again.

Third break: Lunch was perfect. Now for an apple and in about an hour I'll have reached my goal for the day.

I've arrived at the gîte: The last few meters were daunting—the lighter shoes weren't very comfortable. The terrain was too hilly. Tomorrow I'll wear sturdy hiking boots. The crew is the same as yesterday, though another German couple has joined us. I talked with Nicole, the young woman from Switzerland, about us all traveling on in a caravan the next day. Funny, what all happens!

Figure 35: The Australians and the German couple

Daily kms   Total kms

22   518.6

Day 22, Chaumont to Seyssel

First break: I got money and provisions. Now I need to book a room for the night. The only option was a caravan --> check! I texted Nicole that I got a place for tonight. Yesterday evening was harmonious, as was breakfast this morning. I'm glad to be back on the road!

Second break: The first break was only a technical stop, so now is the real break. Nicole has just arrived and is taking a brief pause. She walks so fast. I'm still teaching my brothers about texting. The path, so far, hasn't been tarred and is comfortable to walk on. The birds are singing beautifully up here.

We reached the target for the day, and have the caravan for 20.00 euros.

Daily kms   Total kms

16.7   535.37

Day 23 Seyssel to Crémon

First break: After a fun afternoon with Nic (Nicole) and a regular-sized pizza, we went to bed at 8 pm. Each of us was in their own bed. We are just pilgrims and not a couple! The night was cool and the breakfast meager. Nic left then, and shortly thereafter I did too. After two hours we met up at a rest area and then walked on together. Nic's parents called. They're nearby and bringing a new account card so Nic turn around to meet them.

Second break, lunch: I've found a nice place! Lunch was great, it even included bacon! Nicole met up with her parents and now her mother is walking with her for a bit. I've done also finished lunch and the dishes. One hour lunch break.

Third break: I really needed water and had a small beer in a pub. Soon I'll be off again! I just realized I've lost my "yellow ribbon". It is a pin on my hat that remind me of my comrades in Afghanistan. At least I still have my "Shemag" (a special scarf), it will continue reminding me.

Fourth break: Apple break! The last few kms to the Moulin gîte were hard; I didn't want to walk anymore. It wasn't easy to find the gîte, but eventually I succeeded.

Daily kms	Total kms
26.2	561.61

Day 24 Crémon to St. Maurice-de-Rotherens

First break: The last gîte was super! Dinner perfectly met the needs of a pilgrim: pasta salad with farfalle and tomatoes, then pork chops on warm cucumber, cheese and rosemary. For dessert, cream cheese with sour cream. Very tasty! The garden at Moulin is awesome! A stream rushes down over rocks.

This morning it began to rain, but with no headwind it was okay. The path to the chapel is steadily uphill and demanding. But then it went downhill, which was strenuous and dangerous because the rain had made the earth and roots slippery. I was very glad to reach the bottom and be out of the woods. This way was the most dangerous one I took until now. The forest was beautiful. So many beech trees! But I could not enjoy it.

I'm sitting in a bar in Yenne, taking a break! I almost forgot, along the Rhone there was a beautiful path through woodlands. These woods are full of wild garlic, which is in bloom at the moment.

Figure 36: The way forward & a look back

I was very impressed with the "feel" of everything. Dazed by a very pleasant smell, it's coming back to me now that I'm alone. Nicole is two stops behind me! Indeed, in thinking about the acquaintances of the last few days, I'm glad to be free of distractions again. Thank you!

Second break: Making lunch. The food will be ready in an hour; I must gather wood, prepare and light the fire pit, put water on to boil, and peel and cut vegetables. The place I chose was nice and sunny and I enjoyed this lunch break!

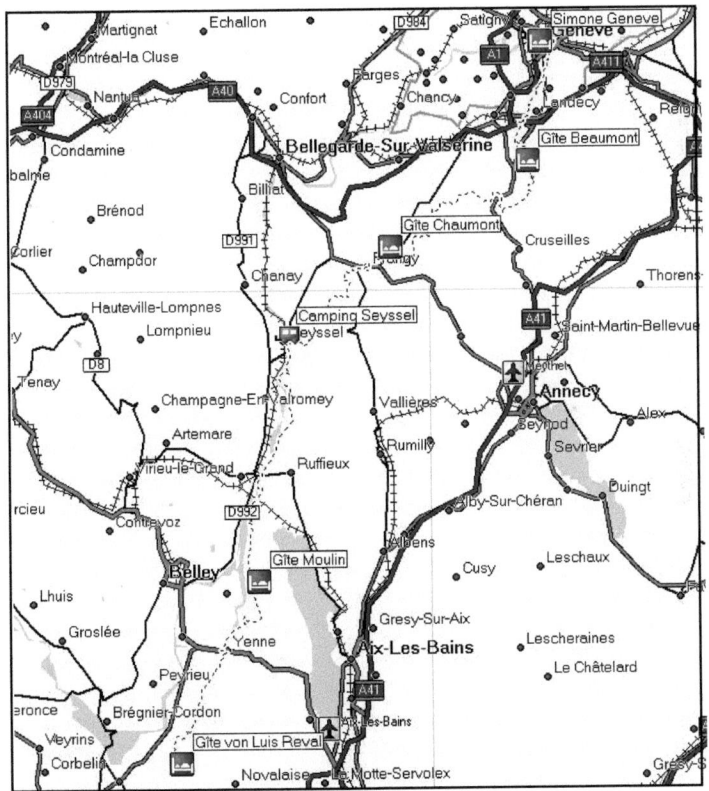

Figure 37: Trail > Geneva - Reval

I chose the easier path, which was a four hour climb to Col de Tournier. According to my altimeter, sea level is at 836 meters, but I'm at 851 meters?

At 5pm I arrived at the gîte. In contrast to yesterday, it is very cheerful here. We pilgrims had a great conversation during dinner. The ski lodge I sometimes stay at in Missen is a little better. Yesterday I was very spoiled. What's important is that I have reached the goal for today. According to the book, I've gotten to St. Maurice de Reval in a couple of stages. How annoying that I now have a blister on the fourth toe of my right foot. I'll keep an eye on it. Oh, the German couple from Montebauer were also here, as are two German-Belgian men who were also in Coumont but couldn't find lodging there. So now I will send some texts and plan tomorrow's route.

Daily kms   Total kms

23.4   585.05

51

Day 25, Easter Sunday; St Maurice-de-Rotherens to Le Pin

First break: The gîte was simple. Louis Revel was a very attentive caretaker, even taking me to his chapel for prayers this morning. The route has been pleasant so far, with the ratio between hard and soft surfaces shifting in favor of soft, in contrast to Switzerland. Earlier I had my first encounter with dogs. Two suddenly ran out from a property and started barking at me! I was surprised that they were Labradors, because my Labrador-Retriever wasn't as aggressive as these two dogs! Yes, this is new on this tour, many dogs behind fences. It's time for a break.

Figure 38: Here is a great place to pause.

I reached Les Abrets, where it is 32°C with a light breeze. I opted to travel to the next town, Valencogne. It's not only my pants that are worrying me now; my left hiking boot is wearing out. Hopefully it'll last through Easter Monday to the next city, because everything is very rural right now!

Break: apple time. My first attempt to get a bed failed, as the number I have is no longer valid. I'll have to look in the next town.

I'm here, but the gîte doesn't exist anymore, and all the others are full! I had to look another 10 kms farther to get a reservation. I've arrived in Le Pin! I did 9 kms farther than planned. I'm once again the only one in the house, but that's okay. I got a very nice room for myself that includes a meal. "Don't worry ..." It appears to be an old farmhouse. The window lintel is, of course, made of wood instead of stone. I'll call Nicole and wish her a happy Easter. Last night I got a bunk-bed for 38 euros including a meal, today a single room with a meal for 35 euros.

Daily kms   Total kms

33.8   618.83

Day 26, Easter Monday; Le Pin to Faramans

First break in Grand Lemps: From now on the path will be flatter. For dinner last night: appetizer, tomatoes with basil sauce and mozzarella, salmon fillet with french fried potatoes, and fresh strawberries for dessert. Mmmm. I am confident that I'll be able to travel as far again today. First I must talk to my wife.

Break: Faramans; lodging is reserved. I'm now accompanied by a 20 year old Viennese girl. It's very entertaining. We discuss politics, the Camino, and the military. She is a student of political science in Vienna.

I've arrived at my B&B and need to shower and then continue patching my pants and update my journal. So now I've showered. I arrived at the lodging at a good time, because now we're having a heat thunderstorm. Nothing wild, but it's beautiful as I sit in my room. Unfortunately, I've forgotten the Viennese woman's name (sorry).

In her opinion, you do not take breaks on the Camino; instead you think, read or write. In other words, you spend time with yourself. That's why doing a pilgrimage is different than just walking or hiking. I think she's right! I, for example, wrote down my thoughts and feelings; most of them, anyway. Oh yeah, I've heard from Nicole. She's in the same lodging that I stayed at in Le Pin. And what did she say, "Christine Grange is very friendly and the B&B is luxurious ..." Now the preparations for Uschi. I promised to send her my coordinates daily. Later I'll send Nicole some information. I need to pause and mend my pants again.

I was joined at the dinner table by a grandmother, her daughter (57) and granddaughter (about 19-20). The granddaughter finished her meal quickly. She was tired because she had been out yesterday, her mother said. I conversed with the grandmother and her daughter in English. The daughter spog Grandmother drove home. Until then we talked about the formation of the German armed forces, and how they differed from the Japanese armed forces. After that, I heard the political opinions of my hostess Later she told me her life's story. The second bottle of wine was empty, and breakfast will be at 7:30 in the morning. So we ended the conversation and went to bed.

Daily kms   Total kms

33.1   652

Day 27, Faramans to Clonas-sur-Varèze

First break: After having breakfast with the landlady I started off again. Nadine de Burler talks a lot and really enjoys it. As a feminist she tries to be independent, but is completely alone. I get the impression that Nadine wants a relationship, but sabotages herself. Assieu seems to be within reach! Lodging information is available at the town's entrance. As it's said, "Don't worry ..." Oh, by the way, I think my pants will last until Le Puy!

Second break: Snack time.

Now the story: It was clear to me that I would try to reach Assieu today. At the second break, I realized that I accidentally took the longer route. My GPS and a Frenchman confirmed that I am on the wrong path. They suggested I reverse my path back to the spring that I passed half an hour ago. I pointed it out to three Welsh-Swiss women who I met along this path. I don't know what decision they made. The Viennese woman from yesterday was sitting at the spring. We exchanged "hellos" and she said she wants to sleep outside today. She was about to formulate another question but saw that I was in a hurry. And so I left. Good thing I found lodging in Assieu; my feet were saying "make it short!" and that's when I saw a notice for a gîte in Assieu. I called them and said I'd be right there. Only the gîte was not between the church and the salon in Assieu like I thought it was, but in Chavanay. And I thought I was on target after 30 km. At the church in Assieu, a mother with her three children was trying to clarify something using my cell phone, but the result was unhelpful. I made a big mistake by following the advertisement! The gîte was actually 15 kms ahead! I was desperate but I had to do the distance!

I had to hike another 9 kms, so I did. I arrived in Clonas-sur-Varèze but, of course, couldn't find the gîte, and even a local man steered me wrong. I looked for a bar to stop and assess my situation! What a surprise! On the door at the bar I saw a St. James shell; did this mean the bar had a bed for the night? Yes! So I ended up at Catherine's store and bar, she prepared her son's room for me while I sat gratefully in the bar. Catherine runs a small shop and bar along with her husband. I was able to take a bath, which helped my feet tremendously. Dinner was filling and plentiful, real home cooking. In addition to the information for my wife I had to warn Nicole that there was no lodging available at Assieu. Uschi would never have let in someone as scruffy looking as me. Some years ago my mother in law also had a B&B in Pfronten. Yes, they always looked for well dressed people who showed they had money! Right then I didn't look nice, I was very exhausted and dirty!

Daily kms	Total kms
39	690.99

Day 28, Clonas-sur-Varèze to St. Julien-Molin-Molette

It's 7 am, and I've arranged to have breakfast with Catherine at 8. Yesterday was really difficult. Blisters developed on my little toes and on the outside of my right heel. They first started bothering me yesterday after my lunch break yesterday, prior to that everything was fine. So now I must orient myself and repack everything. While I was in the bathroom I spotted a scale. Without my glasses I saw it registered 77 kg. – That was a loss of 6 kg!

First break: I'm sitting in front of the chapel of Knights and Horsemen and looking towards the Rhone and Chavanay. A Swiss man, Peter, has also just arrived. He's from Locarno, and wants to pass through here. I think we'll be meeting more often.

Second break, in Bessey: I don't have a goal for the day and don't feel well. At least I've changed out of my mountain hiking shoes and feel better when I sit. Just now an older Frenchman told me, in German, that he worked in Leipzig for two years. I asked if he had to, and he answered no, he wanted to. That must have been before the war, judging by his age. He was very friendly to me!

Third break: apple pause: The shoe change has paid off. My feet feel substantially better; the other shoes need to be sent back to Germany. In Le Puy I'll send the cooking equipment back home, too. The gîte is simple and okay. Peter was already there. I think we'll get along just fine. He has already explored and found a place for dinner. I had to treat the blister today. I hope the rest just disappear, like the previous ones did. Now I'm back on track with the outdoor pilgrim guide. We'll see how it goes tomorrow.

Daily kms	Total kms
22.1	713.11

Day 29 St. Julien-Molin-Molette to Les Setoux

First break: Bourg-Argental. According to "Outdoor" (tour guide) I have reached the daily goal. Yesterday I had dinner with Peter, a retired dentist, and the innkeeper told us we'd easily make it to Les Setoux. That would mean traveling farther for the day's total. Here in Bourg-Argental I'm optimistic. After a simple breakfast at the same gîte, we all broke off, each of us going our own way—everyone has their own pace.

Goal for the day reached: I've arrived in Les Setoux. The band-aid on the blister didn't do its job, so today I have to gather my courage and start walking again. According to the book there are two trails to choose between. The first has two stages, 8km + 16.5km = 24.5 km. Then the other trail's stages are 16.5km + 10km = 26.5km but, in the end, the terrain is more level. I'll decide while walking. All is well today; we are five in the room: Peter, a Frenchman, a German couple from Paderborn and me. The matter of supper and breakfast has been settled. So now I'll read a little and then send some texts. Gîte - 13 euros, supper - 12 euros, breakfast - 5 euros.

Daily kms	Total kms
17.8	730.89

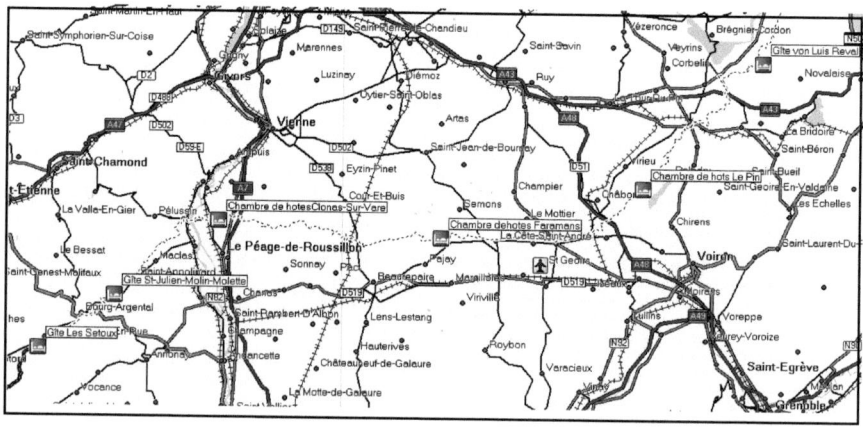

Figure 39: Trail > Reval - Les Setoux

Day30, Les Setoux to La Papeterie

Today is Thomas' birthday; I'll send him a text right away.

First break: Yesterday's dinner was great. Ursula and Wolfgang (from Paderborn), and the Frenchman ate very little meat (veal & liver) so I ate more. Breakfast was served French style: Coffee with milk, white bread with butter and marmalade--> "Ein Königreich für richtige Wurst" (a kingdom for right sausage) in the morning! By the way, yesterday I had to fix my pants again. This pair has to last until Le Puy, there is no alternative. The goal for today is Tence. I've selected a gîte.

56

My lunch break ended at 2pm, so I'm on my way again. While I drank my beer during the last break, a pilgrim walked by, who I had seen taking a snack break before the last ascent. It turns out that he's from the Hamburg area and is traveling the route in stages. From Le Puy he's going to drive to his daughter in Paris. I passed Ursula and Wolfgang before Mountfaucon-en-Velay, but they didn't know if Peter had passed them. I already miss Peter, but he may show up because we somehow decided to meet here. Since lunch the route's scenery has been okay, but I was engrossed by two rumbling thunderstorm cells. The whole time I was looking into the forest for makeshift shelter. When it started to hail I was just passing an abandoned farm and found cover there. After that came a light rain and the thunderstorm moved on. Now I'll go see if the laundry is drying and then put my feet up. I'm in the gîte looking forward to dinner, which will be in 1 to 1 1/2 hours. Lodging and a meal - 32 euros.

Figure 40: Gîte La Papeterie

Daily kms   Total kms

23   754.02

Day 31, La Papeterie to Queyrières

First break: I've arrived in Araules and have decided to climb the peak. After the break I'll reserve lodging. The meal yesterday was great; fantastic salad, noodles with bleu cheese sauce and chicken breast strips, then crème brûlée, espresso, and a cheese platter, which I skipped. I went to bed at 9pm.

I must describe this: around midnight I awoke to find myself sweating so much that everything was wet, and I don't know why. This has been happening since the beginning! For days I have not had to get up to use the bathroom. Why this is happening every night?

Now to Peter—I ran into him this morning while leaving the village of Tence. He walked right past the gîte yesterday and slept in Tence. He's a lot of fun to be with, maybe we'll see each other again on the other side of Raffy. Nicole and Patrick, a companion she picked up somewhere, will probably catch up to me soon, as fast as they're traveling. Yesterday they slept in Mountfaucon. I'll finish my beer and be off again.

I've arrived at Le Fritz. How funny that Peter and Klaus (I met Klaus at lunch) were already here. We are a Triumvirate and I am Benjamin, being the youngest. Of the three of us Klaus is probably the oldest, and often voices his opinions even when we're not really interested. It is what it is. The room is very nice. Everything's new, but in Germany a few things wouldn't be allowed, like the missing stair railings, etc. The view is interesting because I have never seen a landscape like this before. As I came over the hill I was a little overwhelmed ... an ancient volcanic landscape. I am strangely looking forward to Le Puy, a city that will have a post office, etc. Dinner was ready at 6:30pm! We had a radish salad with chicory and croutons, then spaghetti with tomato sauce. I was the chef, so then Klaus and Peter did the clean-up. So now I must send texts to Uschi and Nicole! After this duty we all sat in front of our room and enjoyed the wonderful view down to the Vulcan valley. And of course we had a nice talk about the world and all other topics! A very good night with some great people!

Figure 41: Klaus and Peter after clean-up.

Daily kms	Total kms
19	773.2

Day 32 Arrived in Le Puy; Queyrières to Le Puy-en-Velay

The night was pleasant and the conversation with my roommates was stimulating and enjoyable. For breakfast, the innkeeper brought the three of us the same amount of food as he did when I was alone the day before. I left Klaus in the first large town because he wanted a second breakfast. Peter travels quickly. The earliest I will see him again is in Le Puy. Along the way I met Dietmar again as he was eating an apple. So now we're sitting in a bar together, taking a break, and he is also writing notes. He's traveling this year, photographing all the annunciation scenes in the various churches. How wonderful that my wife called. I just have to pay and then I'll finish the last 10kms!

Figure 42: The first look at Le Puy.

I've reached Le Puy—that's moving pretty fast. I'll take a short break before searching for the gîte. We'll see what happens!

I've found the gîte, but it wasn't easy. It's called the "Friends of St. James". It's exactly where Clemens suggested, how fortunate! Everything is planned for tomorrow, a bus schedule to go shopping and maybe even get a haircut. Then I'll surely find the rest of the things I need and a few postcards. I was sitting downhill from the "Church on the Needle", making plans for tomorrow and the next day, when Nicole rounded the corner with her companion. It was a truly joyful reunion. We've agreed to meet for shopping tomorrow.

Daily kms	Total kms
27	800.24

Day 33, Day of Rest

I took a day to recuperate. It is unusual for a pilgrim to stay at a gîte for more than one night, but I took the break because I walked all the way from home without any breaks. After breakfast I attended Mass, which was very impressive. The Pilgrims left the cathedral on a stairway in the middle of the church which led directly to the Santiago trail! I bought myself new shoes, pants, and batteries. I did some equipment maintenance and sent home some non-essentials. I also wrote quite a few postcards, washed some clothes, and thought about tomorrow's route. So now I'll go to St. Michael's, have dinner with Nicole and that'll be it for the day.

Figure 43: The defective pants have seen their last day!

Day 34, Le Puy-en-Velay to Monistrol-d'Allier

First break: Nicole is with me again. We had dinner together last night, along with a Korean woman Nic brought along. I was in bed by 9:00pm. This morning I misread the clock and got up an hour too early! I was finished with everything before noticing the error, so I went to bed. At 7:00 am, after a good breakfast I attended mass in the cathedral for the second time. That's where I met the little Frenchman from les Setoux.

First break: on the path to Montbonnet we passed a family; a son of about 10-12 years old, another son 7-8 years old, a daughter about 3-4 years old, and a toddler less than 2 years old. The oldest son was leading the first donkey, the mother led the second donkey with the older daughter wrapped up in a wool cloak. The father, holding the younger son's hand, brought up the rear with the toddler on his back. This sight moved me deeply, as I saw pure joy in the eyes of the children.

Second break: Nic and I reached the usual goal for today. We looked at our watches then looked to each other, and decided to continue on to Monistrol-d'Allier.

We've reached the gîte in Monistrol-d'Allier. Nicole and I settled down and ran some errands. This little town has just one very small store for food, without much. The dinner was good, special sausage from this region with mashed potato and white cabbage.

Daily kms	Total kms
29.8	830.69

Figure 44: Some of the family.

Day 35, Monistrol-d'Allier to La Roch

Yesterday's path to Monistrol-d'Allier passed through a fairytale forest, where one must reckon with dwarves and/or fairies! I love forests and if I come through an open wood I start to dream. The gîte was okay; a simple dinner, then I was in bed at 9pm. Uschi really wants a picture of me—maybe Nicole will help me with that. Speaking of Nic, I believe she'll be with me all the way to Chaors. She walks faster than I do, but the paths are about the same length. Now we'll decide where to stay tonight.

Second break: Beautiful picnic spot. Okay, Nic took the picture with my cell phone and I sent it home. Until this break we couldn't find accommodation for the night! First I didn't get any service and then all the gîte were full!

After an anxious wait, I got a call back and rooms for both of us, on the other side of the 1304 m high Col del'hospital. We're now in la Sauvage and still have a 1-2 hour journey ahead of us. Nic is having problems with her feet. The new shoes she bought in Le Puy don't fit well. I hope we do not have to give up too much altitude.

Figure 45: A picture of me for Uschi's cell phone.

We've reached the gîte in La Roch. I recognize a few faces from Le Puy. They all started out on May 2nd. We have to set a goal for tomorrow because the French are still on vacation and lodgings are all reserved. By the way, ever since our "arrival beer", my name has been "Ferdina". I have no idea how they came up with that! Dinner was super: vegetable soup with rice and roast beef, and before, with a salad appetizer and apple pie for dessert. It was very nice to have everybody at the table; from left to right: Nicole, Paggy (French Canadian) a French couple, a French doctor, an English couple with their sister, and plenty of red wine! The innkeeper was very attentive and nice! A great evening!

Daily kms	Total kms
35.3	866.13

Day 36, La Roch to Les Estrets

Nic and I have a short route for the day. We arrived in St. Alban after two hours and reached tonight's lodging at 1:45pm. Nicole must have overdone it yesterday because her feet no longer fit in her shoes and she's in pain. She'll have to buy new shoes in Aumont-Aubrac. Today we're doing a ton of laundry, all done by hand hoping it will be dry by this evening. Since Nicole needs new shoes and will have to break them in, I suspect our days together are numbered. I'm looking forward to Aubrac! Today's path led us through an open pine forest, the likes of which I've seldom seen. In the sun it smelled wonderfully of pine sap. Beautiful!

Daily kms   Total kms

8.09   874.23

Day 37, Les Estrets to Finieyrols

First break: Dinner was good: lentil salad, beef ragout with a tasty sauce and noodles, and ice cream with maple syrup for dessert. I said goodbye to Nicole today; she is having problems with her feet still and hopes to buy new shoes here in Aumont. I think we were both a little sad! Here in Aumont, there is only one ATM and it doesn't accept my card. I'll have to look farther and be more frugal. The barber shop was open, but there were already three women waiting, so I'll just let my hair grow. Shopping is done!

Second break: It's lunchtime, so I'll have a snack. While leaving Aumont I saw Nicole wearing new shoes. She had her happy face on. Then later, who should come around the corner but Nicole. During our conversation, we discovered that we have reservations at the same gîte! So the parting didn't last long!

I've reached the gîte! My room is called "Lys". I reserved a bed for Nicole, too. Oh, by the way, everyone calls my cockade "beautiful flower" (in French, of course, Une Jolie Fleur). Dinner was interesting: salad, mashed potatoes with cheese, egg and garlic, pork roast, and a double crust apple pie in the Aubrac style. The landscape is sparse and romantic but there are flowers in bloom. I get to celebrate spring twice! Narcissus, daffodils, pulsatillas, violas and orchids cover all of the meadows in such numbers as I've never seen. The wind is strong, cold and blows into the room, so we have to turn up the heat!

Daily kms   Total kms

24.3   905.87

Figure 46: Narcissus along the trail, Aubrac

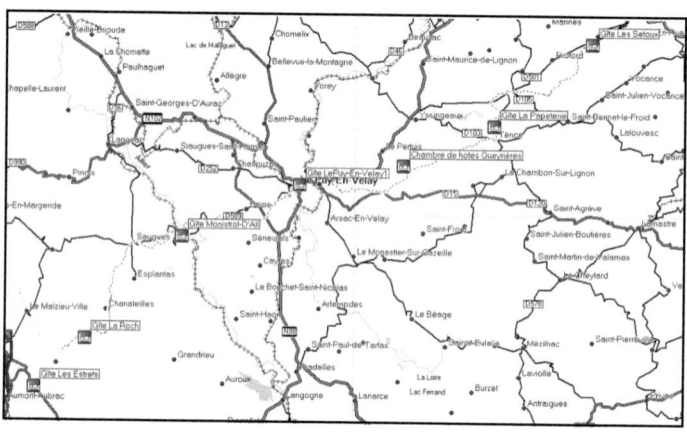

Figure 47: Trail > Les Setoux to Les Estrets.

Day 38, Finieyrols to Saint-Chély-d'Aubrac

First break: Nicole and I finally said goodbye today in Nasbinals. Hopefully we will not meet again on a break! Yes, she was an enjoyable young woman but I want to be alone on my way, I do not need another daughter! I made the sign of the cross on her forehead. We hugged and then said good bye!

My accommodation was 8 km farther than hers. She is a really tough woman!

So now I'll start hiking, so that I don't arrive in Lourdes too late! I've passed Col d'Aubrac. It was the third time that the beech wood indicated springtime with with light green foliage. The route from Nasbinals to Aubrac crossed over a wide Alpine pasture with lots of different meadow flowers: primrose, windflowers, narcissus, bellflower, violas, pasque flowers, orchids (real and pseudo) and some lilies that I don't know the names of. I felt wonderful in this surrounding! All was perfect; the weather, the way, the flowers, the trees just beautiful!

Saint-Chély-d'Aubrac; arrived at the Gîte. So now I'm sitting here with other pilgrims, waiting for the representative who should arrive at 6:30pm so we can pay our bills. What has happened so far? After a shower I went into the village to do some shopping. There I ran into an Austrian couple who I've met frequently on the trail. We drank a beer together and enjoyed an enthusiastic conversation. Soon after, Dietmar came wandering by—nice! Later Dietmar the Oeses (a nickname for Austrians) and I headed for the gîte. When I arrived, I began to cook before the French pilgrims wanted to cook, because by 7:00pm they take over everything, and I'm happy to eat earlier. My pilgrim soup was delicious, as was tomato salad. I ate and cleaned up sat outside on the steps of the gîte. While I sat there, I saw the pilgrims from La Roch again, and a big hello went up all around. How nice, that you always meet again!

The GPS has, once again, turned itself off for 45 minutes. Crap! The night was unpleasant. I am often awakened during the night by my roommates because of my snoring. Sorry, I think they also got a bad night. I can't help it!

Daily kms	Total kms
23.4	929.3

Day 39, Saint-Chély-d'Aubrac to Estaing

First break in Saint-Come-d'Olt: a nice, sleepy little town but I was able to get money. Weather is great, a little bit of chilly wind in the morning, but otherwise a really beautiful Sunday. I took a seat in a very nice bar to enjoy a good coffee! There was a farmer's market in front of the bar. I enjoyed watching people and the whole scene. It was so peaceful on this sunny Sunday!

The GPS has turned itself off again. It's missing about an hour. Irritating! So far the route, according to the book, is 16 km, and not 11.6 km; so 4.6 km went missing. Yesterday was the same. I don't know why?

Figure 48: View of Saint-Come-d'Olt.

Figure 49: View of L'Église de Perse

Second break: Midday in Espalion de Pres. A park along the river Lot invited me to stay and have a break! So I did, enjoying my little snack.

Third break, apple break: I did an additional 2 km loop! Ultreia = always farther. I've arrived at the gîte, which is openly religious. I feel really good. There will be a prayer after dinner, then again before breakfast tomorrow, how nice. It will all be in French, but that's okay.

The dinner was very interesting. First a soup, I do not remember, but the main course! Noodles with ham, this is also usually at home, but I never got raisins in this meal!!!! A new experience! After dinner all the pilgrims do the dishes. Everybody wanted to help, but nobody was drying the plates. So I formed everyone in a production line, which ran smoothly!

Unfortunately, I could not send Uschi a text because there is no reception. I was also unable to book the next night. The people here booked the next gîte for me.

Daily kms	Total kms
25.1	954.39

Day 40 Estaing to Sénergues

First break: Golinhac: the day started with prayers and then a meal. After the third bite of jam-topped bread I switched to a butter and salt topping instead. A Frenchwoman (from Alsace, who spoke German) announced to everyone present that I miss my sausage and cheese for breakfast. Everyone was surprised! Different countries different breakfast!

The damn GPS has turned itself off again. Instead of 16kms (according to the book), it registered only 10kms. It surprised me that I hiked the distance in 3 and a half hour despite the marked gradients. And I was not the fastest one on the path.

Now that I am somewhat rested, I'm enjoying the very impressive view of the church's square while drinking a beer in the pub and put my legs resting up on a chair. What a great feeling!

Figure 50: The view!

Some thoughts ran through my brain. One was that my backpack is still too big! I plan to buy a smaller one if I get to Toulouse or Lourdes, but I won't tell Uschi. I know that she won't like this!

Second break: I think I'm 2-3kms away from my goal for the day. I'll eat a small snack.

I've reached the gîte! I did my laundry, showered, and planned my lodging for tomorrow. Now I'm sitting on the terrace admiring the view. I must hike 29 kms tomorrow, because there are no closer accommodations listed. In the guide book, I discovered a song that reflects my mood well. "Thank you for this good morning ..." I often sing it while hiking. It makes me feel good, even when I repeating it!

Daily kms	Total kms
21	979.49

Day 41, Sénergues to Decazeville

First break, Noailhac: the last gîte was pretty expensive. Little food, and the wine cost extra!!! And breakfast wasn't to be served until 8:00 am! At 7:00 am I heated my coffee in the microwave! I was so glad to leave that gîte. The hike so far has very nice with great weather. After the break the path headed towards Conques. The city was very narrow, and the trailleading to it very steep. The front of the cathedral was a great place.

Figure 51: Portal of the cathedral in Conques.

Figure 52: Conques: The path down to the Dourdou river.

To cross the river Dourdou you have to go further downhill. The path to Conques was okay, but then I left the valley ... I'm thankful that I've often been in the mountains and can handle slopes, because leaving the valley was another steep hike! I was very exhausted when I reached the top of the hill!

I've reached the gîte in Decazeville. The path down here was pretty exhausting. Only downhill on paved roads! Now my laundry is drying in the sun. I visited the tourist office to ask about the train schedule to Tarbes and also about a barber. After a moment of consideration, I realized I can get to Toulouse by foot, from Toulouse to Tarbes by train, and then walk from Tarbes to Lourdes. The way to Bach is clear, GR 65 (this is the name of the Way of St James in France) and after that I'll make a new plan. I need new maps! 1:100,000 scales would be nice. I'll sit here until 5:30 pm when I have an appointment with the barber and do my notices. By the way, it's 33°C in Decazville.

This was my first haircut in France, and I was surprised because the lady led me to the sink even though I just showered an hour ago! But she washed my hair anyway which felt really good. A lady's hand on my head! I think she did a good job on my hair as well as my beard.

Daily kms	Total kms
26.5	1005.98

Day 42 Decazeville to La Cassagnole

Oh yeah, yesterday I lost my clip-on sunglasses. My trip to the barber was very pleasant, almost as good as in Sardinia. I've planned a route to Lourdes, and finally found a map with a scale of 1:100,000 in a stationary store. I'll stay on the Way of St. James route until shortly after Bach, after which I'll head towards the south.

First break: In St Felix, and the only bar is closed! I'll dig into my bread bag.

Second break: Finally, a beer; I think I've earned it! It must be at least 30°C in Figeac. I've reserved lodging, and have actually found the way out of Figeac. It was not easy, because there are signs leading into the city, but not out again.

La Cassagnole; gîte reached: during the last few meters I passed a struggling Frenchwoman. I had to keep going, so I informed her with a mix of gestures and words that she shouldn't have both poles at her sides at the same time. She should use them like walking sticks and move them forward alternately. That took about 20 seconds. Later, she came to the same gîte and thanked me profusely! The guidebook says there are no meals here, but the first question was would I like something to eat. Yes! I couldn't find a grocery store in Figeac. Now I must plan for tomorrow.

Daily kms	Total kms
32.6	1038.6

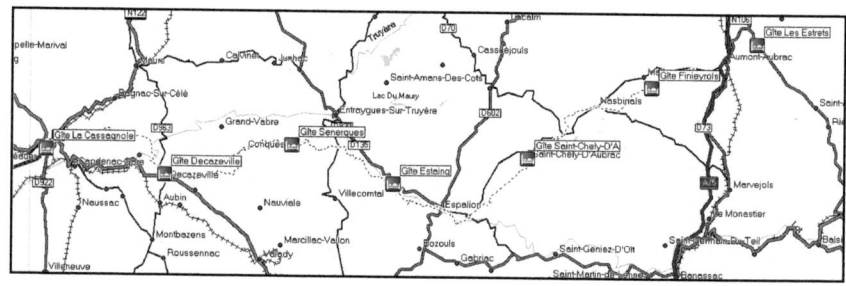

Figure 53: Trial > Les Estrets to La Cassagnole.

Day 43, La Cassagnole to Gaillac

First break: Dinner yesterday was okay. I got a salad with raw duck breast, roasted duck leg with potatoes au gratin and a nice chocolate cake for dessert. This morning I thought it was raining, but the sun bright.. It is cloudy though, and not as hot as yesterday. Now I need to think about my goal for the day!

Second break: still no goal! There is a city nearby and several km farther a nice town, what should I do?

Gaillac: I decided to stay in this little town. I've reached the gîte! My goal for the day has worked itself out. The washing machine is running (using curd soap sliced into the washing machine with a vegetable peeler). I am clean and going to town, but there isn't a bar! The gîte is an old house. I'm staying in the parent's bedroom.

During my first break, I saw the Frenchwoman with the poles again. This time she had opened the tap screw too much, but I was able to help! She looks like she has an eating disorder, she's extremely thin.

Nicole texted and said that she'll be taking another day off because of her feet. I hope she'll be able to finish her journey.

After hiking for awhile I arrived at a town called Faycelles. It is a sleepy town and not very interesting. As well as some other villages, it's an old one. But the path out led to a very impressive sign! You see it on the pictures below. It was a great motivator that I really appreciated Yes, I know that whoever wrote this doesn't know me, but it was still very to see! A big smile spread cross my face.

Figure 54: The front of the sign & the back of the sign.

3 kms before Grealou I heard footsteps behind me. A Frenchman, who was at least 65 years old, shot past me carrying just as much weight as I am! I was very surprised!

Now I'm waiting for the washing machine to finish and making plans for tomorrow. I also read the New Testament. And Uschi, of course! The daily information about my target and that I am still alive. There came a knock on my door, and the innkeeper was there with a bottle of red wine and a hunk of bread. The bounty was mine for 1.5 euros. That saved my evening.

Daily kms	Total kms
29.3	1067.94

Day 44, Gaillac to Vaylats

First break: Limoges-on-Quercy: Uschi wanted to know about the traffic jam on the Middle Circle (this is a saying in German that refers to the fat of one's belly, like a "spare tire"). I must have sunken cheeks; everyone wants to give me bread. It was foggy this morning, probably because of yesterday evening's downpour. I left at 7 am and hiked through the oak forest.

The bird on the path is in no hurry to fly away, so I'll take a longer break! Now the landscape has changed into a very dry and calcareous soil, or so I've read. I love oak trees; there are three of them in my property. I wandered through this area with a big smile on my face, and the solitude made me so happy!

Second break, midday: About 8km after my snack, I allowed myself a beer. It feels a bit strange now to orient myself toward the south. Today I've only seen one other pilgrim from afar. I believe I'm totally out of sync. Regardless, I'm looking forward to Lourdes and new bed sheets. I decided that I won't buy a new backpack. I'll repack it in Lourdes!

I've arrived at the "Sisters of Jesus" in Vaylat, which is the last gîte on the GR65. Starting tomorrow I don't know where I'll eat or sleep. But "Don't worry ..." Mass takes place at 5:30pm, I'm looking forward to it. I've washed the clothes, the boy is clean, and the bottle of wine from yesterday is empty. Tomorrow I need to carry my backpack more across my shoulders, because it's chaffing my right hip. I'm anxious to see how that helps.

Here in Vaylat I will part ways with Gabriele. He and I have met often since Finieyrols! His English is almost non-existent, and my French equally poor. But there was one scenario where we actually understood each other! He had trouble with a piece of his equipment and I was able to help him. On another day I procured food and drink for us. Yes, this has been a very good time but now it is ending.

Figure 55: A bird on the path.

Daily kms	Total kms
29.1	1097.07

Figure 56: Gabriele and I saying farewell at the monastery!

74

Day 45, Vaylats to Caussade

First break, Caussade: I've just eaten some meat and French fries after hiking. They tasted great! So now I have to wait until 2 pm when the tourism office opens.

Yesterday at the monastery, the sisters served cassava soup, green bean salad, Spanish style rice (paella) and cordon bleu (frozen food, heated in lard). The rice was great! Tonight we had a thunderstorm with intense rain. It rained all day long with varying intensity, and only stopped shortly before my destination. I am totally drenched! The Goretex isn't water proof, I think, or maybe I sweat too much, but I'm going to have to buy a raincoat.

The tourist office has opened and I booked lodging and dinner for 70 euros. Too expensive, so tomorrow I'll have to be frugal. Now I am all clean, and there is a heater in the bathroom which I hope will dry everything by tomorrow. Supposedly it will be summer again! The path here followed the road because I had no other information, but I have a few telephone numbers for Montauban. The map designates a bike path, so I think I'll take that way. That was all for today.

Daily kms	Total kms
26.4	1123.68

Day 46, Heading for Lourdes; Caussade to Montauban

First break: yesterday's dinner was so-la-la! The wine was good, but scarce. The food wasn't worth mentioning. The conversation was in English, and the hostess' husband only listened. The clothes dried, thanks to the heater in the bathroom (at 70 euros I didn't feel guilty). This was the most expensive night I've spent on this journey!

Second break: Montauban railroad station: I think I'll have to get a hotel room and continue my journey tomorrow. I walked another 10km with no lodging in sight. I stayed here in Montauban and it was a very inexpensive hotel. I've just spoken with Uschi on my cell phone, both important and unimportant things, "TradGem", my club at home. Nice information but not important.

The news about our friend Suzanne L's illness really brought me down. I don't know what to do about it. Pray? I'll do that and hope. "Don't worry ..."!

I'm hungry and trying my first "croque-monsieur". Because of my last visit to France with my VHS class (an adult education school), I know what toasted ham and cheese is called here. I won't have it again. I didn't like it.

Daily kms	Total kms
26.7	1150.37

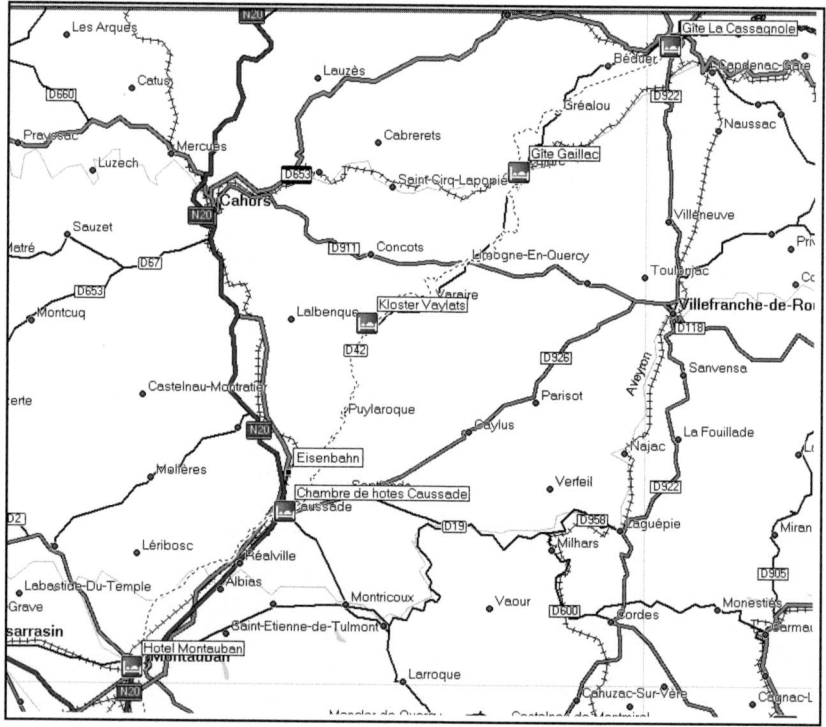

Figure 57: Trail > La Cassagnole to Montauban

Day 47, Montauban to Toulouse

First break; Corbarieu: I have the necessary maps now and can plan the route to Lourdes. I'm feeling pretty good now, not only because I needed the maps, but also because I just really love maps!

Second break: tuna in salt water with bread. After lunch break I looked for the tourist bureau. I found it in the winery after 45 minutes of walking — closed on Monday! So, I'll go back to the mayor's office at the village. I had to look for it, too, but found it after another 45 minutes of walking around. The office is located in the Hotel de Ville (this means "town hall"), interestingly. I didn't know that the town hall was called "Hotel de Ville", I was completely confused there were no office hours listed. No one is in the street! But on one corner I saw the bus schedule and was able to figure out how I will go to Toulouse, though I'm still somewhat doubtful.

I finally believed it in the moment that other people arrived at the bus stop! I took the bus to a metro station at the city limit of Toulouse, then the metro to the main train station and looked for a hotel. The cheap, 1-star hotel is in the Red Light District, which is not okay for me. I was able to use the automated ticket machine for the regional trains, hurray! I also bought today's newspaper in German. Then I looked for a bed. I found one and it was not too expensive.

Now I'm happily sitting at a street cafe and enjoying it! I walked around for a bit in the Old Town (the ancient heart of this city). I wouldn't want to live in this city; it would be like living in a museum. But there is more happening here than in Munich or Zurich! It somehow has a Mediterranean flair, wich made it more appealing. This made this big city more sympathetic

The plan for tomorrow: take the train from Toulouse to Boussene, walk to St. Gaudes, and then get lodging.

On the following day: take the train from St. Gaudes to Tourney, and then go by foot to Tarbes! On 5/19 I'll go by foot from Tarbes to Lourdes, by way of Bartrès. This is the plan, hopefully it goes smoothly..

Daily kms	Total kms
65.1	1215.7

Figure 58: The road to Corbarieu.

Day 48, Toulouse to St. Gaudes

I've reached Boussens by train, now I'll continue on foot. Walking out of a big city like Toulouse is unpleasant, and Lourdes is still two days away. But now I am back on the busy road. After 2 km I was able to turn right and came to a nicer road with less traffic. The sun was shining and my mood was perfect.

I took my first break before a tough stretch. I entered a bar and had a coffee and a little cake like a muffin. There were some old French men and took their with morning aperitif, a nice glass of white wine! What a nice scene to observe. After this break the road led into some ups and downs with some great views!

Second break, some lunch. Yes, I changed my eating style. From Switzerland through Le Puy I ate lunch as my main meal, and now I have just a small snack. I feel better eating the snacks because my stomach isn't overloaded.

Figure 59: A tin of fish with bread and warm beer.

Third break: banana break!

I've obtained lodging! The underwear is washed, and so is the man! All is well. It's a good thing I learned to sleep anywhere when I was a soldier! I'm glad Klemens gave me a fitted sheet to take! I bought some bug repellant in one of the earlier gîtes. The shower was dirty, so I cleaned it! This accommodation is the grossest, dirtiest one I ever had! Nicole took a break for a day and is unhappy because her legs are still hurting. To take a day off means you can't walk, and that feels strange after all this time. I'm sitting in the church's square, enjoying it. The church appears to be genuinely Romanesque. Tomorrow I'll take a picture for Klemens. He loves this kind of church.

Daily kms   Total kms

92.6   1308

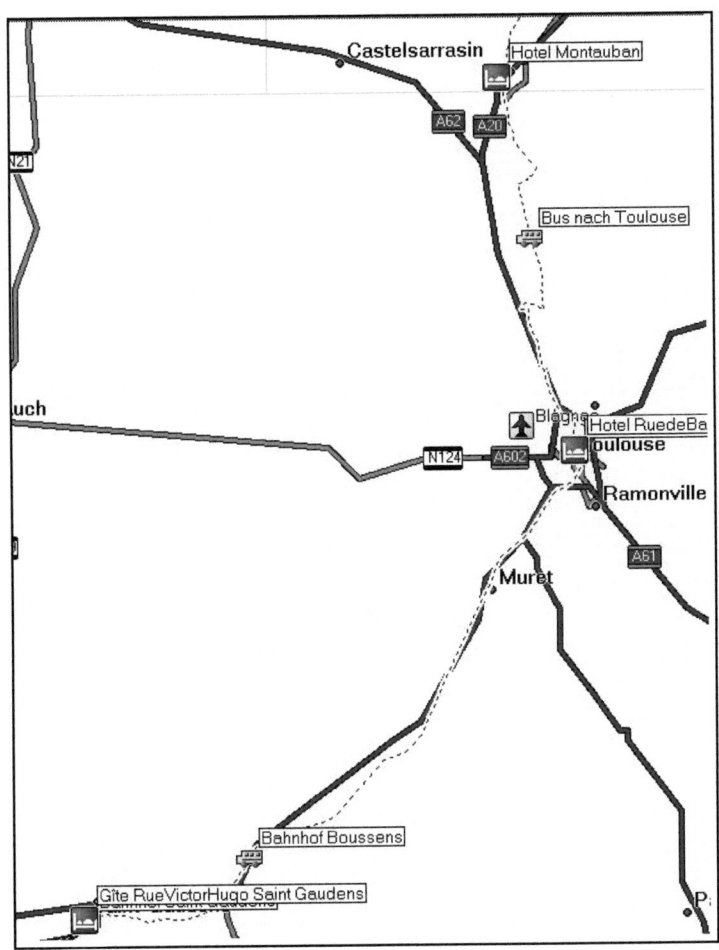

Figure 60: Montauban to St. Gaudes.

Day 49 St. Gaudes to Tarbes

I paid 10 euros for this accommodation, and even that was too much. I walked to the train station. I'm back on the train now, heading towards Tourney and then I'll continue on foot.

First break: finally, breakfast in a bar in Bordes. It's 8:50 am and the French are already having an aperitif! A nice white wine! I had my breakfast with coffee and a muffin!

Second break: A beautiful view of the lake! I had a longer break and also enjoyed a little meal. I took this picture knowing that I will cross these mountains, the Pyrenees!

Figure 61: Lac de l'Arrêt darré

Third break: a beer; I'm almost in Tarbes!

At the tourism office in Tarbes, I obtained lodging in a monastery. The town is called Laloubère; I'm south of Tarbes. After a two hour wait, the priest arrived and showed me to my room. 22 euros for an overnight stay with dinner is okay. We'll see what else is available. A storm is brewing to the south. It will probably thunder soon in Lourdes! It would be nice if everything blows through by tomorrow.

Daily kms   Total kms

75.8   1384.09

Day 50, Tarbes to Lourdes

Last night's dinner was sparse and lacked wine. I conversed with a student in English. The breakfast this morning! "Farmer's pole" (granola bars in the Swiss dialect) were on the table. This was not enough food..

The path to Bartrès was strenuous. Along the highway to Lourdes --> pure stress! Heavy traffic on both sides of the highway! I tried to find an easier way and headed round the airport, but no success! So I had to go back to this busy road! Horrible!

I hiked half the distance to Lourdes when an off-highway option appeared in the form of a beautiful wooded path. But the map and the real world disagreed. I got completely lost! I didn't know where I was and I just tried to find a way out of the forest. My GPS didn't load the right map. Oh well; "Don't worry...!" in the moment I said this sentence in my mind, I saw an exit from the forest! I couldn't believe it!

Another good hour and I'll be at my destination!

Figure 62: In Bartrès

I've reached the train station in Lourdes. A special train is already here, one from Bavaria. The pilgrims are already at the hotel. The greeting committee is still there, waiting for the next train! I presented myself to the First Sergeant, who initially stared at me with his mouth wide open when I told him I started in Germany. But then I got my welcome drink. It's customary to greet the pilgrims with music by the military Music Corps and a cup of red wine. I got a few cups!

I've arrived at the hotel, woo hoo! It all worked out as planned. I saw many familiar faces and big hellos from those who know me. The atmosphere is captivating. It's pleasant to be out of uniform. Oh yes, in uniform, one is an ambassador of one's country and must act in an appropriate manner. It is easier as a civilian.

I bought an umbrella and took my first walk through the city. Laundry was in the washer. My cloth sleeping bag is finally getting washed, too. 30 days and nights is a long time. Now I started on the mail. I wrote a lot of postcards. The atmosphere in town is really nice as well.

Daily kms	Total kms
24.4	1408.5

Day 51, Day of Rest!

Today I'm resting! Yesterday I took the Stations of the Cross alone, unfortunately, because it was raining lightly. The way was pretty emotional. At every station some memories entered my mind, recalling to me some situations that I endured omn my journey from home!

Today there was a German trade fair at the Lourdes Grotto, after which I did what I always do in Lourdes—go to the castle. It's always lovely to look out over the city from way up high. The garden with its model homes is always worth viewing, and each time I discover something new.

Finally, I've bought the ticket for tomorrow. I'll ride as far as Pau and then, via bus and train, to Somport pass, because the weather forecast is very bad and I don't know the correct path to cross the Pyrenees.

I refilled my water reserves at the spring. It can't hurt to have holy water on a pilgrimage. Carola, an official secretary from my former airbase, and I had a good dinner with all the other pilgrims at the hotel. She helped me organize my time in Lourdes and she also looked for my Spanish package. Like in Geneva, I sent new clothes, Spanish tour guide and maps down to Lourdes with a comrade. They also took my French package back to Germany.

The evening ended joyfully!

Figure 63: Carola (assistant parish of Kaufbeuren) and I at dinner.

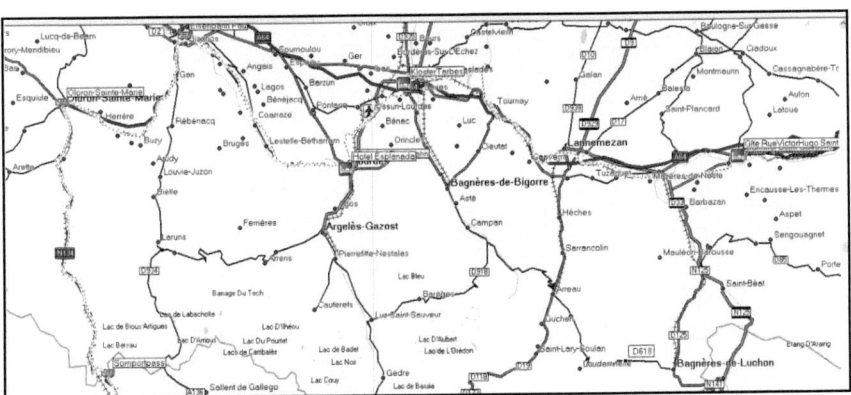

Figure 64: St. Gaudes on Lourdes to Somport pass.

Day 52, Arrived in Spain; Lourdes to Villanua

There is nothing else to say about Lourdes. I was sitting at the station waiting for the train to Pau. Yesterday was a good day with lots of variation. The travel passes quickly; I am in Pau now and have my ticket to Somport! The Pyrenees are shrouded in fog!

I've reached Somport pass, the sun is smiling from above, and I get to experience, spring again. How amazing this is!

Figure 65: First sign in Spain

Figure 66: Distance to Santiago de Compostela

Figure 67: Now I'm in Spain for the first time.

My first refugio in Spain is completely different than in Cuckoo-Land (France, where every day I heard a cuckoo calling). Cost for bed and a meal, 25 euros.

It feels good to be back on the road. As nice as it is to meet some people I knew, it's hard to take a day off.

The refugio is clean, and I can send some texts. I also did my errands and wandered around the village. I was the only pilgrim here but some locals were also in the restaurant for dinner, which was okay, and red wine was included.

Daily kms   Total kms

164   1572.01

Day 53, Santa Villanua to Cilla de Jaca

First break: Jaca; breakfast--> very lame; cold coffee without milk, just muffins, not a good start to the morning.

The route to Jaca was pleasant. It'd be nice if it continued this way. In Spain on Sunday, it seems that the world stands still!

I passed through Confranca-Estation yesterday! A huge train station, but no train tracks, and the public places were very expensive. There were hardly any other people around. Many apartments are empty! A sad place!

Second break: I was sitting in a rest area and enjoying my lunch of canned fish, a piece of bread, and some refreshing water.

Third break: arrived at the hostel in Santa Cilla; the route remained pleasurable. I found the refugio right away. It's pretty orderly.

A guy from Mannheim, I think his name was Fred, passed me on my first break. I've known him from our bus ride up to Somport pass. He practically ran to Jaca yesterday. His goal for today is Arrès. It's supposed to be really nice there, but I was not walking one more kilometer! If I can keep a pace of 25 kms per day, I can be home for Richy's birthday.

By the way, Carola cornered me about a family weekend of Catholic military pastoral care, where I could talk about my experiences during this journey. I said yes, but not before February 2012, with my wife of course!

This afternoon I did my homework at the only bar in town. Suddenly a group came in! It was a loud crowd with a boisterous mood! They came from Cologne, Germany, a jolly group. They rearranged the chairs and tables to their liking. Yes, I talked with them and we laughed a lot together. After an hour or so the tour guide pointed out that the bus had arrive, and everyone was ready to run out. I had to remind them that they should clean up (the tables and chairs), and they did it!

There were also two Polish women who were walking the path for the second time. One speaks English well, the other German. So I switched back and forth between the two and then everything got translated into Polish. How amazing this situation was. Dinner was simple, the wine light and the company merry.

Daily kms	Total kms
28.9	1601.07

Day 54, Santa Cilla de Jaca to Ruesta

First break: no breakfast so far. I'm glad I was able to get coffee and a chocolate croissant at a bar here in Ponte la Regina de Jaca! I bought some bread and snacks at a gas station. The goal for today is Artieda.

Second break: tuna with bread. I met a young Austrian couple who are hiking the Camino in stages. It was a nice conversation.

I've arrived in Artieda, but it's too early to get lodging. I've decided to continue to Ruesta. The route to Ruesta is beautiful, and for a while travels through a very pleasant forest. All is well and good, but with the sun burning down and having walked 37 kms, I would like to finally reach my destination! In this wonderful forest I met an Italian pilgrim. He was very exhausted so I shared some water with him because he was running out. Yes, it was a very difficult hike to Ruesta and after another 2.5 kms I finally stepped out of the forest and looked up to see it. Ruins!!!!!!!

Figure 68: The path ahead & behind

Figure 69: View of Ruesta

My tour guide book says there are supposed to be 40 beds here but this is the scene that greets me after 40.8 kms. Where are the beds? After rounding another curve, I came to the well-equipped Refugio with a nice waitstaff and a good dinner.

Daily kms	Total kms
40.8	1642.02

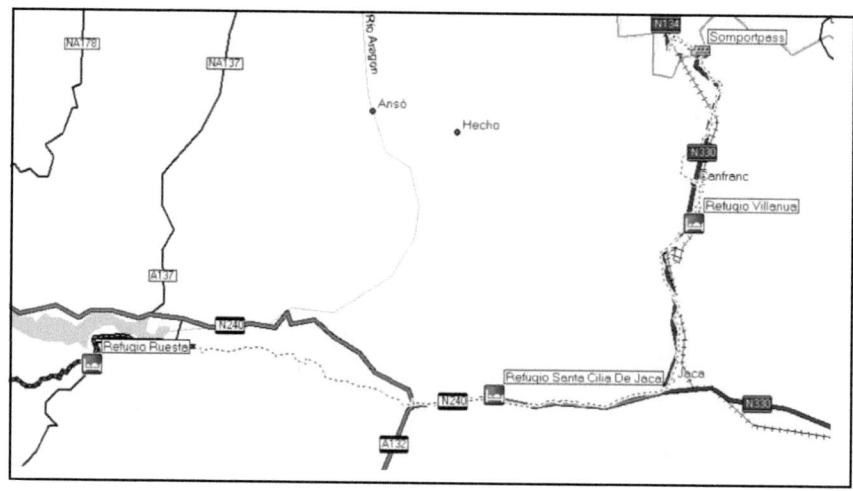

Figure 70: Trail > Somportpass - Ruesta

Day 55, Ruesta to Sangüesa

First break, Undues: a supplement to yesterday in St. Cilla, a quote by Hans from Berlin: "Traveling by foot is the only real way to travel, even a bicycle is too fast!"

Now about yesterday - Fredy, the long haired bomber I met on the way to Somport, was also there. We had a brilliant conversation about philosophy, esotericism, religion and social politics. Afterwards, along with some Spanish girls, we formed a circle and massaged each other shoulders. Dinner was great; roasted pork! Unfortunately, breakfast doesn't begin until 8:00 am! That's too late. I think I'll get up with the sun at 6:30 and be on the road by 7:15 am. That's my plan for now.

Today's goal reached: Sangüesa; the hostel is okay, 5 euros but no food. I arrived early enough to visit the church and go shopping. I'm well prepared for tomorrow. I had tuna for breakfast, with milk to drink. Tomorrow will be strenuous, two passes to cross and I'd like to get as far as Monreal! Fredy and I are going to dinner tonight! Eating out was not a good idea for us. It's only 6:00 pm and we're hungry, but nothing is available until 8 pm

! So we went shopping! The picture shows the results:

Daily kms	Total kms
21.3	1663.88

Figure 71: Morning stretching with the Spaniards.

Figure 72: Fredy and I enjoying ourselves

Day 55 Sangüesa to Monreal

First break: the first pass, I pause for a banana. Today I've got great weather again, sunny and warm! The way was wonderful after I left the industrial area of Sangüesa. The trail leads along ruins that were established by Francis of Assisi as he traveled to Santiago! It was a small monastery.

Second break: I've reached Izco. All I can get here is something to drink. It's a Refugio without a bar. Bad luck! I'll continue on to Monreal. Here in Spain there are a lot of swallows. Even during my youth in Kaufbeuren, I did not see as many as here. Seeing them made me a little happier!

I've reached Monreal: I found the hostel, which wasn't easy. I was too late to have lunch in the community room, so I'm doing laundry and reading - I'm making good progress in this book. The supermarket doesn't open until 4 pm Fredy is here too, he went through the Vulture Gorge. The Spanish girls are also here with their friends. We're all going to dinner together. A fun evening!

Daily kms	Total kms
27.4	1691.33

Day 56 Experienced a Place of Power; Monreal to Puenta la Reina

First break: Tiebas, the path here was exhausting because I climbed too far and ascended an extra 100 meters for nothing! The Refugio was already bustling at 5:30am. And I thought I was up early! The Spaniards on pilgrimage are really active!

Second break: The Church of Saint Mary of Eunate!! First I had a banana break! Then I went into the church—it stirs the soul—one is not alone in struggling with emotions or expressing them. After my own experience I saw some people with the same reaction as me.

Then I walked barefoot around the church. It was so different, bringing both good feelings as well as bad feelings. In the tour guide it is written that you should do it three times. In some spots it was quite pleasant, but in others my feet really hurt! I don't know what this means. I was only able to do it twice. Every part of my body reacted differently. Yes, I was quite confused. I'll have to come back to this place again and try it a third time.

I also met Fredy again. He was already exercising in this powerful place. I think he is very happy. I won't see him again.

Figure 73: Eunate, a place of power!

Traversing through Puente la Renia, walking through the town was very strange. The town is separated by a straight alleyway, and the pilgrim trail goes passes many enticing bars. I wanted to settle my accommodations first. At the end of the ally, I didn't see the bridge!! A passing Spaniard pointed me in the direction of the gate. Then I recognized it—this was the way across the Arga River.

Here was Fredy again in my mind. I think he's comfortable in Eunate, though I'm glad our paths have parted. It's enriching to meet other people, but it's also good to part paths and do it one's own way.

The Refugio that I've reached after crossing the bridge is more like a factory farm! Chickens should not be kept like this. Even former military conscripts in the army had 9.2 meters at their disposal. Food will be served at 7:00pm today; we'll see how that goes. I don't remember what I ordered other than salad and chocolate mousse. Now I'll plan for tomorrow. I'm on the "Camino Francés" now.

Figure 74: Puente la Reina

Daily kms	Total kms
32.3	1723.69

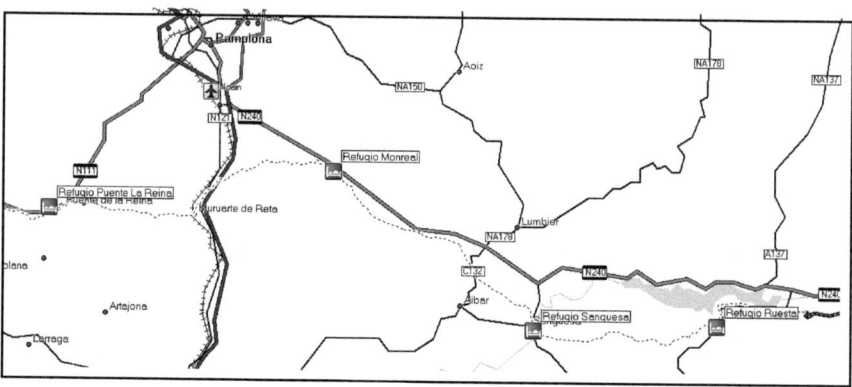

Figure 75: Trail > Ruesta to Puente la Reina

Day 57, Puente la Reina to Los Arcos

First break: the night at the chicken farm was okay and the dinner, too.6am I was on my way again! Yesterday I talked to someone who was from Eastern Germany and now lives in Frankfurt/Main. He was very obese and extremely tired. He's been on the route since Pamplona and was very emotional. He couldn't connect with his wife via cell phone, and that (along with his cumbersome weight) exacerbated his exhaustion. I tried to encourage and advise him, so I hope he takes my advice. "The Way gives you what you need!"

The road to Estella was not particularly demanding. It is now only 11:30am, so I'm going to continue on to Villamayor de Monjardin. The weather is okay, with some clouds and a temperature of 15.5° C.

Second break: Lunch in Estella; here I am, lost of course. I finally found a bar and bought some snacks. Sometime after lunch I found my way out of Estella. The path led uphill, and a group of people suddenly emerged through a gate. I was curious, so I looked in and discovered a source of wine. A young man was standing at the tap, drawing a glass! Super! I entered and drew a glass of wine for myself. I wanted to sleep in Villamayor, which wasn't far away. I meant to drink the wine while writing that night; fantastic idea! The young man turned out to be from France. I asked him to take a picture of me. I emptied my water bottle and filled it with wine. Awesome! When I reached Villamayor, I met the Frenchman again and he pointed out that the hostel was already full, and the other hostel no longer existed! Solution - go on to the next town!

That would be Los Arcos, 12kms further, but the road was filled with people! All the people who couldn't get a place were continuing on the same path as I. The question then became, how many accommodations are available in Los Arcos? So I had to really pick up the pace and pass a few people who might get to a bed first. I remembered my time in the military, and those marches. Every year we had to do a march in a set time. I learned to increase speed during downhill trails. I also thought that I was well trained after more than 1700 kms. So I ran down every hill! That was how I meant to get a bed in Los Arcos! Only the bicyclists made me nervous. I was no longer thinking "Don't worry …" Along the way I came upon an Austrian woman whose backpack was all askew. I tried to help her and straightened it out a bit. Maybe I should've stayed with her longer, because I found out later that she needed help again. I arrived in Los Arcos and found accommodations in the Casa Austria. After setting up my bed, shopping, and taking care of hygiene, I treated myself to the wine in my water bottle. Wonderful!

Daily kms	Total kms
42.8	1766.51

Figure 76: The wine tap & drinking wine

Day 58, Los Arcos to Logroño

First break: Viana: All I had for dinner was a can of sardines! Later I conversed with a woman from Styria/Austria about all sorts of things. We talked a lot about the grandkids and some other topics.

I can feel the last 40 km from yesterday in my bones. It's still 10 km to Logroño, where I hope to find a Refugio.

The difference from the earlier areas: In Germany I was all alone, there were a few pilgrims in Switzerland, and then from Geneva to Le Puy it was pleasant, from Le Puy to Vaylat strenuous, from Vaylat to Lourdes lonely, from Somport to Puente la Reina active, and from Puenta a full-scale pilgrim migration!

I've reached Logroño! On the paved road at Logroño's entrance I started feeling pain in my left shin. I think it's just muscle pain from yesterday, because my thigh is sore too. I won't think about it anymore! I remember that many people quit the Camino due to periostitis of the tibia. The route into the city was really dragged out. I barely secured a bed at the Refugio!

Daily kms	Total kms
27.4	1793.98

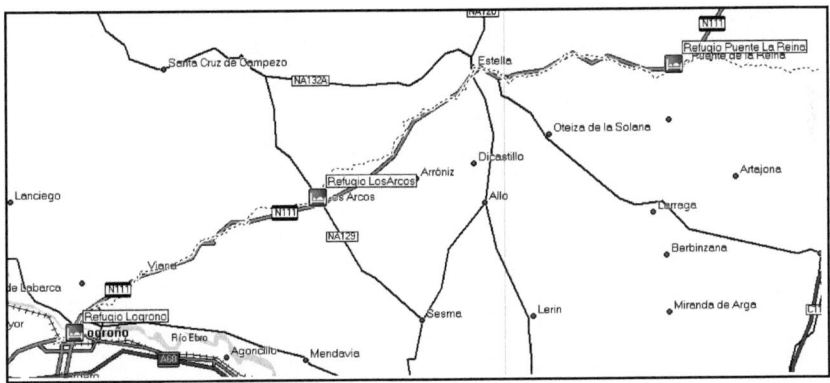

Figure 77: Trail > Puente la Reina - Logroño

Day 59, Logroño to Nájera; Here my reason for walking

First break: Navarrete; It was a restless night. The victory of Real Madrid in the championship league was celebrated Saturday evening until the early hours of Sunday morning. The streets were still full of revelers when I dashed off at 6 a.m. In the bunk above me was a Brazilian woman who spoke fluent Portuguese, Spanish, English, and German with a Bavarian accent! A likable person! I met her again later, but she had to break off and fly home. During this break is when I first met the Alaskan ladies. Later we were often in the same town.

Second break: Ventosa; I ate fried eggs and bacon - delicious! It was the first time since before 3/30/2011. A woman named Annette (Franconian) sat with me, and we talked while I ate. She was having a quiet day and an American had just ordered a taxi for her. On the way to Nájera one passes a wall upon which the following is written in Spanish and German:

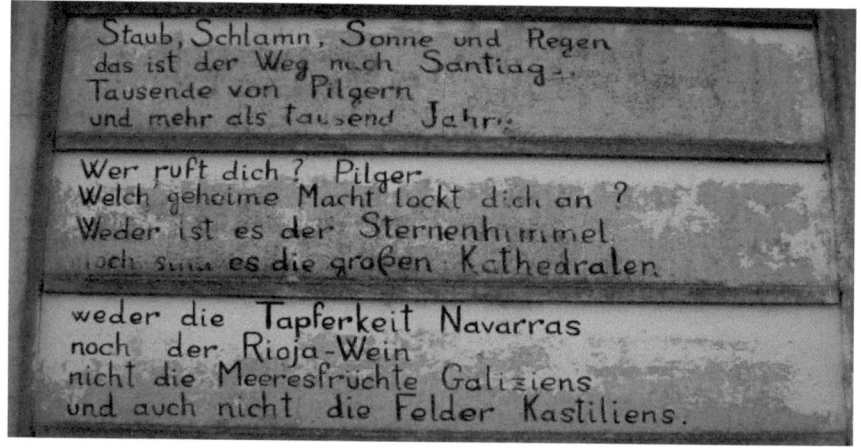

Figure 78: Part one

Dust, mud, sun and rain - This is the way to Santiago.

Thousands of pilgrims - And more than a thousand years.

Who calls you? Pilgrim - What secret power lures you?

It is neither the starry sky - Nor the great cathedrals

It is not the bravery of Navarre - Nor the Rioja wine

Not the seafood of Galicia - And not the fields of Castile.

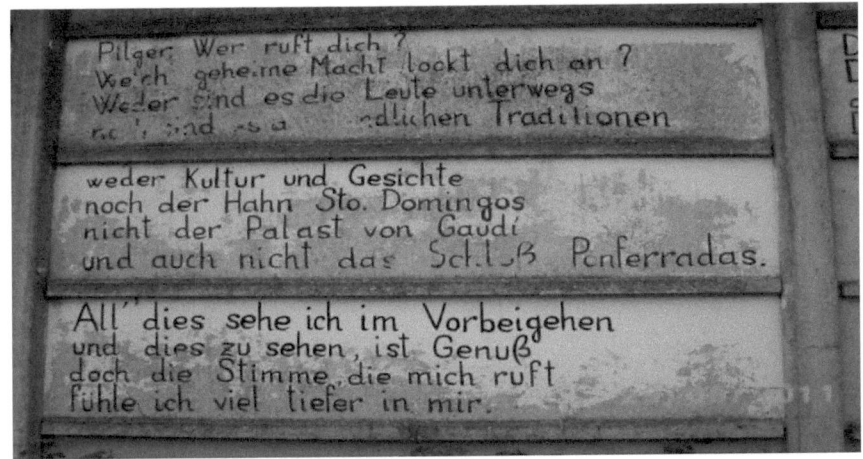

Figure 79: Part two

Pilgrim, who is calling you? - What secret power entices you?

It is not the people on the move - Nor the universal nightly traditions

Neither culture and history - Nor the cock of Sto. Domingos

Not the palace of Gaudi - And not the Ponferradas castle.

All this I see in passing - And to see this is pleasant

But the voice that calls me - I feel deeply within myself.

Figure 80: Part three

The force, which drives me forward.

The power, which entices me

I cannot explain it further.

Only He above can do that!

Poem by priest Garibay Danos

It moves everyone who walks past!

I've reached the Refugio: it's a dormitory with 80 beds, two showers, with two toilets for men and two for women. I could not have traveled the next leg even though it was a distance of only 6 kms. The muscle in my left shin is screaming. Before I reached the hostel, I went into a pharmacy and bought ointment with arnica and alcohol. Hope dies last! I hope there isn't inflammation in my shin. Now I'm sitting at a table in a bar, drinking a beer. There is an outlet for my cell phone, hooray! There are no outlets in the Refugio, and yesterday and today there were only outlets in the laundry rooms! After a dinner in the bar of seafood paella, I sat in the refugio, drinking wine with the Frenchman and another young man. We had an interesting discussion about our European community. It is touching to hear and understand the opinions of young people from other nations. I asked them both to continue expressing their critical ideas for Europe in their hometowns.

Daily kms   Total kms

29.7   1823.68

chicken miracle

*The so-called "**chicken miracle**" of Santo Domingo de la Calzada is closely associated with the legend of St. James.*

At the height of the Santiago de Compostela pilgrimages, a pilgrim family came from Xanten to Santo Domingo de la Calzada. One night they stayed at an inn.

The landlord's daughter was attracted to the son of the family. He was pious & chaste & rejected her offer. The attraction of the landlord's daughter turned to evil wrath. She sought revenge & hid a silver cup in his baggage. The landlord noticed the loss the next day & sent for the town constable, who quickly found what was missing. The young man was hanged after a short trial. The parents continued on to Santiago with broken hearts.

On the trip back home, they came by the place of execution where they spoke with their son, who wasn't dead because he was held by Santiago (version 1), or Santo Domingo (version 2). The parents ran to the judge, who was sitting down to a meal of fried chicken, & told him what had happened. The judge replied that their son was as dead as the 2 chickens in front of him. Suddenly, the chickens came back to life & flew away. Then the son was "unhung" & the landlord's daughter was hung. The family returned home.

This legend exists in many versions in relation to "the Way of St. James". Artistic references relating to the miracle appear again & again.

Source: Wikipedia

Day 60, Nájera to Grañón

First break: Azorfa; had breakfast in a bar. My left shin is really painful, so we'll see how far I can go today. My walking speed is significantly slower and I am applying ointment often.

Second break: Cirunuela; I've passed a vacant new home area into the old town and the only bar. I make frequent stops now, hoping that it helps! The bar has just opened and reeks of cleaning fluid! Regardless, I go in and sit down because I'm very sweaty. I ordered beer and a bocadillo (a Spanish sandwich)! Cold beer for my shin to cool it and the bocadillo for my hunger! The pain in my leg is slowly subsiding. I hope I make it to St. Domingo.

Third break: On the way down to St. Domingo de la Calzada, I was in so much pain that I had to stop here. I'll go see the two white hens in the cathedral for 2.50 euros, and then look for lodging. Then I'll start for home. (Author's note – the pain in my shin was so horrible that I thought I would quit here). My shin has put me in a bad mood! I stayed in the cathedral and prayed for awhile. I ignored the museum and the trinkets and went over to my backpack. Now find a bar where I can get a beer and figure out how to get home. It was not easy to find a bar but I managed it. I ordered a large beer and thought about the day's possibilities. When I looked down I was astonished to see that the swelling in my shin was significantly reduced and the pain had lessened. I was thinking about giving up, but now that is impossible to imagine. What happened? Prayer? Such a change could not happen by just icing and applying ointment. Prior to St. Domingo my left leg had about 15% of its capability, now it's over 65%! I'll drink another beer to that! Fantastic, because I was ready to give up! I was already thinking about how to get home. Can it be that the cathedral visit and prayer have brought about this miracle?!?!

I canceled all thoughts about going home and looked forward! Yes, I'll reduce my hiking speed and take more breaks. This was my decision, so I'll head to Grañón!

I've arrived at the hostel in Grañón: the bed is very simple, consisting of a thin mattress on the ground very close to a fellow traveler. Holy Mass is at 7 pm, followed by a communally prepared dinner. I'm looking forward to it. The dinner was very good and I got a lot of conversation. It was a very pleasant pilgrim night.

Daily kms	Total kms
29.3	1853.01

Day 61, Grañón to Villafranca Montes de Oca

First break: Last night was really fun. To my right sat Karin from Belgium, to the left sat Lindsey from Alaska, and opposite me was a young man from Ireland! We had a great conversation in German (Karin) and English (Lindsey and the Irishman). What more could one want from life? Another reflection was offered after dinner. I did not take part. Neither did Annette or Wilma, so the three of us finished off the wine! It was great. But earlier in the evening was a pilgrim Mass, ending with a pilgrim blessing! As the say in the Allgäu: "First Mass, then a liter of beer" (Erst die Mess' und dann die Maß). In the afternoon I spoke with an elderly German man who had spent much time in Spain. We spoke of the real estate bubble here and the changes in the landscape! He was very troubled by it. He was also of the opinion that walking is the only way to travel. I almost forgot about my left leg; no more thoughts of quitting!

Second break: Belorado; I'm singing in the rain. My left leg feels perfect again! I am so happy!!! I'm the only one singing on a bad road in lousy weather! The road is covered with red dust which sticks to my shoes like cement. Step by step it clumps on my shoes until it finally falls off and I am walking one-sided. That was a tough road to travel.

Third break: Villambistia; I finally got something to eat. Here I met a small group from Biberach, a town near Memmingen, my hometown! We had a great chat and exchanged our experiences!

I've arrived at the hostel: Villafranca Monte de Oca. It only rained once today, sometimes more, sometimes less. The 6th day of rain on my whole trip! I don't have enough songs! I would recommend others to take a harmonica along. I also stopped and did my homework (writing in my travel journal and texting my wife). Not far from the hostel I ordered food from a pub's pilgrim's menu. I sat at a table with Ralf and Herbert. One is from a region outside the city of Bern, in Switzerland, and the other is from Schleswig Holstein. While talking, I learned that the one from Holstein had my late Uncle Karl as a gym teacher. How small the world is.

The Spaniards had closed all the Refugio's windows. The air was like an animal cage!

Daily kms	Total kms
30.2	1883.46

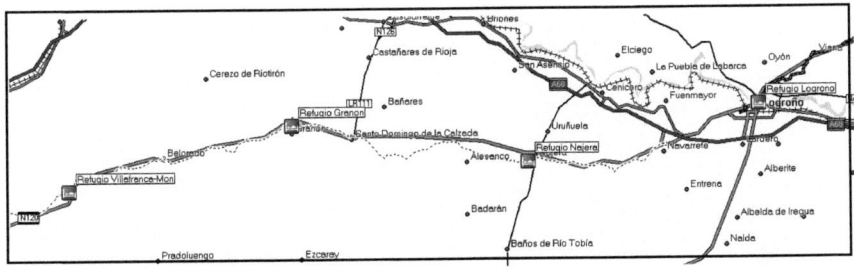

Figure 81 Trail > Logroño to Villafranca Montes de Oca

Day 62, Villafranca Montes de Oca to Burgos

First break: San Juan de Ortega; the weather is perfect, not too hot, not too cold, and the sun is shining! I'm writing my notes. The Alaskan girls are also here. They'll leave soon, but maybe we'll meet again. My plan is to find accommodations before Burgos, and then tomorrow I'll continue through Burgos and then find another Refugio.

Second break: Cardenela de Piopico; this is where I wanted to spend the night, but the hostel no longer exists. I went to a bar, ordered a beer, and swore into the air. The host and a patron were also present. The patron asked me if I started out from St. Jeaen-Pied-de-Port, and I told him I started from my house. He didn't believe me until I showed him my pilgrim pass! I didn't have to pay for my beer!

I had to go into Burgos, first around the airport and then the long road through the industrial area to the town center. Near the airport I met the Alaskan ladies, who were tired and sitting in the street. They felt the same as me, only without the beer break!

Third break: I've circled the airport. An entertaining scene is happening in front of the pub: A bus is just pulling away when the driver spots two female pilgrims. He opens the door to allow them on. The ladies pointedly turn away in the opposite direction, ignoring his offer. The driver shakes his head and drives off. Who were the women? The Alaskans, naturally! After the break, I too was also on my way. My left leg is still okay. I can feel it, but the breaks and the slower pace are helping. Oh, there are the girls again; we went to the city center together. They are just as tired as I am, and six eyes can see the yellow arrows faster than two.

Figure 82: Debra and Lindsey

We've reached the hostel: I'm assigned bed #622. We arranged to meet for dinner. I went into town to buy batteries and provisions. Then I sat down in a bar to do my homework. I haven't finished creating a plan for tomorrow yet!

Daily kms	Total kms
36.9	1,920.4

Day 63 Burgos to Hornillos del Camino

First break: Tardajos; I left very early this morning so that I can walk slower. The crowd has already passed me. That's okay though. Oh, by the way, today is Ascension Day, and also Father's Day (in Germany). Richy called me and my wife sent me a text. Great! Last night was really nice I had a great conversation with the Alaskans. Debra is 50, and Lindsey is 54. Both are married with grown children and a teenager still at home. The dinner was also very good. Afterwards, we walked back to the Refugio together. The bus scene evoked hearty laugher a few more times. The ladies had no idea they were being observed.

I checked my GPS and noticed that I walked slower than before. This pace is good for my shin 4.8 km/h on average is pretty good. The innkeeper gave me a parting gift of a Madonna pendant. After the hell in Sto Domingo I was now in a good mood, thinking I would reach my goal --- Santiago!

I've arrived at Hornillos del Camino, but the hostel isn't open yet. Ever since Burgos there have been lots of pilgrims on the road so lodging will be scarce. The hostel is open now, and will fill up quickly. I got a bed and my clothes are in the washing machine. I've got a little time to think about the previous evening; the Alaskans want to sleep here. They gave me their pilgrim passes so I could check-in for them, which was fortuitous because they got the last two beds.

My plan for tomorrow is to hike 30 km to the next hostel. The terrain profile looks very easy, just one hill and the rest is level. I'm sure I can manage it.

Tonight we're going to eat dinner together again. We were joined by a Canadian couple and enjoyed a very animated conversation during dinner. By the way, practicing English has increased my language skills. But I am still not perfect!

Figure 83: L to R: me, Lindsey, Debra, the Canadian couple

103

Since we were the 6 pm shift, we had to leave to make room for the later shift, so we went to a pub. We sang songs with two people from Holland (about 60) and a German woman. It was another great pilgrim evening!

Figure 84: In Vino Veritas, singing and laughing!

Daily kms	Total kms
20.5	1,940.93

Day 63, Hornillos de Camino to Itero de la Vega

First break: Hontanas; reaching this first break was a lonely route of cornfields, nothing but cornfields. Then finally, a cup of coffee with something sweet! The coffee perkedme up, but everything else was so exhausting. I remember last night happily. It was really fun with the two Dutchmen who were great singers.

Second break: Castrojeriz; parting hasn't happened. Now I'm traveling with the Alaskan ladies, which is great. During the day it's every man for himself. At night, people meet up again and sometimes go to dinner.

Third break: at some point after the hill. Some Spaniards were offering fruit and drinks for a donation. I took a can of beer and left a sufficient donation. Beer was just the thing after a long, hot stretch!

Figure 85: The Alaskan girls ahead.

Figure 86: It goes downhill here.

Itero de la Vega: I've arrived at the hostel! Oh, I got a bed that creaks with every movement! I don't have a clear goal for tomorrow, as there are still questions about lodging, etc. The next town will be the last before another long hot stretch.

Daily kms   Total kms

34.2   1575.11

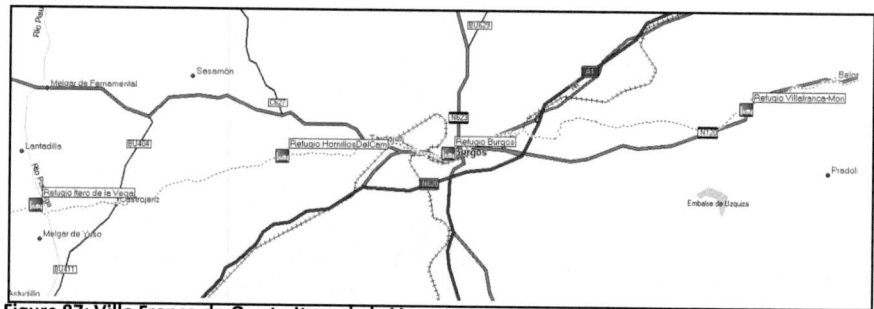
Figure 87: Villa Franca de Oca to Itero de la Vega

Day 64, Itero de la Vega to Carrión de los Condes

First break: Formista; the day was great and I didn't allow my thoughts to wander to my shin! I was very happy about that!

Second break: Villacázar de Sirga; my shin? I'm not sure why, but now it only twinges when I put a lot of strain on it. I'll see how it progresses. I'm staying optimistic and looking forward!

I've reached Carrión de los Condes. All the hostels are full so I'm at a hotel. The Spaniards are good at business; a room with 3 beds is allotted to 3 people who each pay 17 euros. So I'm in a room with a Dane and a Norwegian woman! It's almost like being in a hostel, except that the bathroom isn't shared by 50 or even 100 people. Today's route was moderate, and my left shin is getting better. I think it will heal if I stick to this slower pace. According to the GPS I've just crossed the 2000 km line. That's a reason to celebrate, right? Since the Alaskan ladies are staying here and are the only people I know, I invited them to join me for a drink. After dinner we went to a bar and drank to my 2000th. Now I'll make plans for tomorrow.

Daily kms	Total kms
33.7	2008.84

Day 65, Carrión de los Condes to Terrdillos de Templarios

First break: Calzadilla de la Cueza; straight ahead was total sun and tons of people on the trail for as far as the eye could see. I paid attention to the tips and brought along plenty of water, which I really needed. In the bar I got a good farmer's omelet. It was just what I needed after that last stretch. I didn't pause along the way, and only drank from the water containers. This break was wonderful and I felt renewed.

Terradillos: I've arrived at the hostel. Thomas has been in touch and sent me a great plan for my return home! Here it is --- Santiago to Porto by bus, and from there a plane directly to Memmingerberg. This plan sounds perfect! The question now is when will I be in Santiago? We must start planning! Debra is having problems with her knees and is talking about taking a day off. We'll see what happens.

Daily kms	Total kms
27.2	2036.33

Figure 88: An interesting depiction, Jesus is blonde!

Day 66, Terradillos de Templarios to El Burgo Ranero

First break: Sahagun; Yesterday I experienced an outpouring of grief and emotion. I had to leave the room to be alone with myself. It passed after a rough 20 minutes.

Second break: Bercianos del Real Camino; lunch time; I must say some things about yesterday. Dinner was okay. At the table were Annamarik (from Holland), three Frenchmen, the Alaskan ladies and I. The conversation during dinner was trivial but entertaining. Little by little the table emptied until the only ones left were Annamarik, Lindsey and I. We got into an intense conversation. My mood was somber due to bad news from home (about the deaths of some friends, Lutz, Hirsch and Florian, and also Susanne's cancer). Annamarik managed to coerce my emotions out with all her questions and rhetoric. I hardly lasted 15 minutes before I had to leave the table. I excused myself and left, feeling very emotional, to take a contemplative walk. I was very angry with that woman. Sometime later I spoke with Lindsey about the experience and began to feel calmer and more grounded. This morning my feelings are sorted out again. In retrospect, I'm very glad I had the encounter with Annamarik; it's good to be brought back to reality. I'm thankful to her and Lindsey for lending me an ear. I feel lighter and happier!

I've taken quarters in El Burgo Ranero, though there is only room for me to have a folding bed. I've completed my homework and met Juergen (the tall German) again. We had a good discussion, mostly about religion. Before that I tossed my laundry in with that of the Alaskan ladies and they took care of it!

Daily kms	Total kms
31.2	2067.49

Day 67, El Burgo Ranero to Puente de Villarent

First break: Reliegos; It's rained almost the entire day. Debra has stayed back. She has a problem with her knee and can no longer keep up the pace. I talked with Lindsey about the history of Germany. She asked where the colors in our flag come from. I told her the story, starting with the war of liberation against Napoleon, continuing with the "Hambach Festival", the Weimar Republic and ending with the Federal Republic of Germany. Later we were passed by a bicycling pilgrim who was displaying Bavarian and Augsburg flags. This fit perfectly with our theme, so I called to him "Hallo Datschiburger!" which is the nickname of the city of Augsburg/Bavaria/Germany. He stopped of course, so we took a break together and talked a bit about his route, where he started, how far he plans on going, etc.

I've arrived at the hostel in Puente de Villarent. By dinner I had finished my plan for tomorrow. I'm going to quickly cut through Leon instead of hiking along the N-120. I'll take the more scenic, albeit longer, route through Villa de Mazarife! The Alaskan ladies decided to stop in Leon for provision. This will put some distance between us.

Daily kms   Total kms
19.4   2086.96

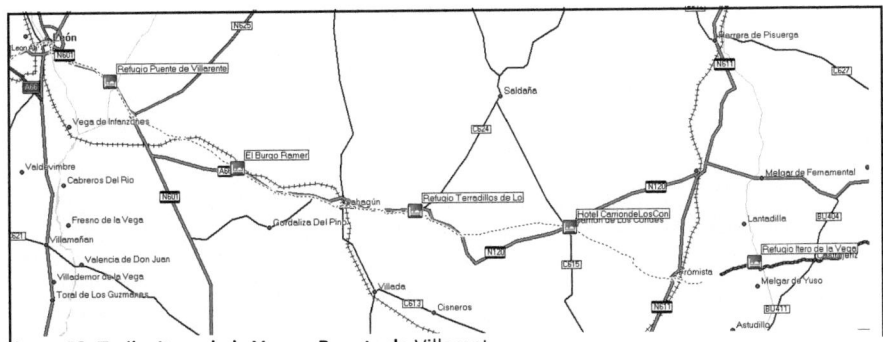

Figure 89: Trail > Itero de la Vega – Puente de Villarent

Black, Red, Gold

Main article: ***Black, Red, Gold***
The origin of the colors black, red & gold is to be found in the liberation wars of 1813 against Napoleon Bonaparte, namely in the uniforms of the Lutzow Free Corps. The Corps consisted mainly of students who came together against the occupation of Germany by France (see also the first student fraternity). The volunteers came together from all parts of Germany under Prussian Major Adolf von Lutzow. They brought with them differing uniforms & civilian clothes. The only way to bring uniformity to their attire was to make everything black. Added to this were gold buttons (brass colored) as well as red lapels. To popularize this account, these colors contributed to the flag of the Holy Roman Empire.
This color scheme is also confirmed by a historically authentic saying from the wars of liberation:
Out of the blackness of slavery through bloody (red) battles to the golden light of freedom.

Source: Wikipedia

Day 68, Puente de Villarent to Villar de Mazarife

First break: Leon; I got really lost and only found the path with the aid of my GPS. I enjoyed a good coffee. After that I went to the cathedral, and there again, emotions ran deep. Klemens called! I told him he is always with me.

It was difficult to get out of Leon and my mood was lousy, I don't know why. The weather was great and my plan seemed pretty good, but I walked out of Leon with my head in the clouds. I crossed a street and did not realize that the traffic light was "RED" for pedestrians! I walked right into the busy traffic without thinking about it! Thank God that the driver saw me in time, otherwise I would be in hospital or even the grave yard! I felt the car bump my left leg! I apologized profusely with a very big THANK YOU to the driver! I was still alive!!!!

Second break: Chozas de Abajo; I stopped in the one and only bar. The route was extremely lovely and pleasant! The Spaniards enjoy an extended lunch hour. A group of four men are sitting in front of a rose' wine and an ample meal.

Little Julia, my second grandchild, has a birthday today so I've already called her. I think that made her happy. In any case, Diana was very surprised.

I've arrived at the hostel in Villa de Mazarife. The Alaskan ladies are far behind. I have some time today for my finger and toe nails! I've decided on a departure date—June 25, 2011, so maybe I can still walk to the End of the World! Uschi and Thomas have been informed. I hope Thomas will be able to book me the flight from Porto to Memmingen.

Supper was good, and once again many nations were represented: Italians, Canadians, Frenchmen and Hungarians. I conversed with a Hungarian sitting to my left. When he heard my name he became more talkative because the first Hungarian king was named Stephan. He railed against the apostle Paul because he was first in line at the stoning of Stephanus! The Italian group was also very friendly. I was curious how often we'll meet each other along the way. Also, I've met a fellow from the Saarland. Most of them started in Leon. All beginners! Ha Ha Ha! I felt like an advanced hiker while the others were all "Greenhorns"!

Daily kms	Total kms
33.6	2126.85

Day 69, Villar de Mazarife to Santibánez de Valdeiglesias

First stop: Villavante; I had to walk a straight path on asphalt all day today. Yesterday's route was nicer. It was so boring, to see the road as far as the horizon!

Second stop: Hospital de Órbigo; I ate lunch here in this town. An elderly couple entered while I sat in the restaurant. The man wore a kilt and the woman a causal hiking dress. When he left briefly I asked the lady if they were from Scotland. The lady said no, they were from Australia. This was the second time I met Australians along this Journey!! She told me that his ancestors were from Scotland and he knew the entire history!

I've reached my daily goal: Santibánez de Valdeiglesias; the hostel isn't open yet. There is no bar in this village, just a social establishment which is similar to a bar but is maintained by volunteer citizens who determine its hours. They are all very friendly!

I got a bed once the hostel opened. The garden is amazing! So many fruit trees in such a small space! Every tree had an attached notice stating that it had been sprayed. The landlord, Hercules, wrote this out just for the pilgrims. At any rate, I felt like I was in the Garden of Eden. The hostel was full, but supper was great. There was a jolly group of ladies from Austria. We all laughed a lot throughout the dinner. About the meal: a very tasty risotto with porcini mushrooms! The main course was fried chicken with Italian fried potatoes. Plentiful food and good wine! A successful pilgrim evening!

Daily kms	Total kms
20.2	2147.65

Day 70, Santibánez de Valdeiglesias to El Ganso

First break: Astorga; today is another warm day. On the way here I passed a rather strange snack stand. A selection of juices and teas as well as fruit and coffee, all for a donation! The character who manned the stand sat in the likeness of an Indian, wrapped up in a blanket! He was completely lost within himself and hardly seemed to notice me. I was thankful for a cup of coffee and put a coin into the box.

Second break: St Catalina de Somoza; I ate lunch here. I had a tin of fish, some bread and water.

I've reached the day's goal: El Ganso; two bars stood side by side! I opted for the bar on the right. I found the hostel after a lengthy interval and reserved my sleeping place. The Alaskan ladies were also in the hostel, so we all went to dinner together.

Figure 90 : Dinner with the Alaskan ladies in El Ganso!

Daily kms   Total kms

25.3   2172.36

Figure 91: Trail > Puente de Villarent to El Ganso

Day 71, Cruz de Ferro; El Ganso to Riego de Ambos

First break: Rabanal del Camino; it is a cool but nice morning, perfect for the way up to the "Cruz de Ferro". After breakfast I retrieved the stone I brought from Memmingerberg from the recesses of my backpack and wrote on it. This is a tradition for the pilgrims, to take a stone from your home and write on it. I scrawled the thoughts the flooded my mind!

The way has, so far, been moderate but now climbs steadily uphill. The first goal for today was the cross, and my thoughts wandered to the importance of it and what it meant to me. I am a bit perplexed, confused and not at all sure what I will find at the top. I will soon know.

The path becomes steeper and is now further away from the street, a beautiful trail. The cross comes into view. I am a little nervous! I put down my backpack and wait in line. There are already a few pilgrims here, and the sun is shining in a cloudless sky. Everyone can take as long as they want in front of the cross. There is no rush and no crowd, just tolerance and understanding all around. I was still waiting in line when I was in position to climb the little hill beneath the cross. I sat down and held the stone with the words on it in my hand. I felt good! Suddenly my surrounding no longer existed. For just this moment, I was completely alone in the world!!! What was going on here? The stone was still in my hand, I glanced at it then threw over my shoulder. Then it started again, endless emotions washing over me! My smile ran away from my face and tears were falling! I didn't understand it but I was very glad that it happened!

Figure 92: I'm still laughing at the Iron Cross! But ...

I don't know why but it was a blissful sensation!!!
I took a little pause off to the side.
The pause ended and the descent began. I had lunch in Al Acebo. A
wonderful bocadillo with scrambled eggs and bacon with a refreshing beer! It is
amazing how many people I have seen again! Oh, it's wonderful that everyone is in a
good mood and no one had a bad experience!! Conclusion—the Camino gives you
exactly what you need!

*The **Cruz de Ferro** (Iron Cross) is a small iron cross mounted on a tree trunk, marked in the Montes de Leon, at 1,500 msnm, the highest point of the Spanish pilgrimage route on Monte Irago. (Only the Somport Pass on the Aragonese path is higher).*
The cross stands in a pile of stones which is continuously enlarged by the pilgrims. There are covered resting places for pilgrims next to a small, modern chapel. Prior to Christianity being introduced to this town by a hermit who erected the forerunner of the aforementioned cross, it was common for people to pay homage to a Roman divinity by leaving behind a stone. This would not have been the first cult in this spot as the Celts used road crossings & other natural formations as places of worship. According to the warden of the pilgrim hostel, Tomas from Manjarin, the pile of stones has been heaped up over the past 50 years to make the locale easier to reach by bus. The original pile from Roman times was always 300 meters from the road. In the 1990s, the Cruz de Ferro felt victim to vandals when it was cut through by a chainsaw.
The original custom of leaving a stone was not part of Christianity but has now been integrated into the pilgrimage. A stone, brought from home, served as a symbol for the "sins" left behind by the pilgrim after catharsis. Many pilgrims use the Cruz de Ferro to leave behind personal items, letters or even votive offerings.

Source: Wikipedia

I've reached Riego de Ambros and found a very nice, communal hostel! Dinner was in the company of a frustrated, elderly German man! It's a shame to be so negative while traveling! He gave a glimpse into his life, and it was clear he was struggling with many things. He has a heavy load on his shoulders and I hope he will find a way out! I have a different opinion now, but at the time I passed judgment! Now I regret doing that!

Daily kms	Total kms
27.5	2200.1

Day 72, Pentecost Sunday; Riego de Ambos to Cacabelos

First break: Molinaseca; I ate breakfast. This town is idyllically situated along a river, how great! It looked a little like the towns in my home region. The people here planed ahead for the tourists and I think they did a very good job! I had a good breakfast and the surroundings gave me peace.

Second break: noon; in Camponaraya; my left shin did superbly on the ascent! I think it was back at 90% on strength. I will continue walking slowly. It is Palm Sunday and the weather is pleasant again. By the afternoon it was really warm!

I have arrived at the hostel: Cacabelos; the cabins have two beds but they can only be locked from the outside! We are certainly less than 200 km. from Santiago. We meaning the Alaskan ladies, me and all the other pilgrims in town! Funny, we seem to following a pattern to Santiago. We don't see each other during the day, except perhaps at lunch, but our goals are often the same! Tomorrow I want to get as close to the pass as possible!

Oh, yesterday there was an encounter with three large dogs that were blocking the path. They allowed cars to pass but not pilgrims, so I searched my memories for a way to pass. Dogs always look straight ahead and they don't understand an ace pitcher! I took some stones from the ground and threw them at the aggressive dogs. I was unable to hit them, which was fortunate because I didn't want to hurt them. The dogs didn't understood what happning, but they moved out of the way!

Daily kms	Total kms
27.4	2228.08

Day 73 Pentecost Monday Cacabelos to Herrerias

First break: Villafranca del Bierzo; a nice place, good weather, what more could you ask for to accompany a great breakfast of fried eggs and bacon!

Second pause: a rest stop where I eat an apple and a banana! There is nothing more to tell.

I've reached the hostel! Full! Herrerias; I have to go to a guest house. It will be more expensive but I'll have a room for myself as well as my own bathroom. In particular, I'm looking forward to a new towel! Nice! Besides which, there is a good pilgrim menu at this guest house!

I used the time until dinner to do homework sitting by a bubbling stream, which could just as well be flowing in the Allgaeu. It felt great to be in that pleasant atmosphere.

Daily kms	Total kms
29.3	2257.37

Day 74, Herrerias to Tricastela

First break: O Cebreiro; the climb up here was quite steep at times, and still foggy at the beginning. Further up, a light wind blew the fog away. The view was amazing on top of the pass. When I got to the pass I treated myself to a well earned breakfast of freshly squeezed orange juice, coffee, and fried eggs with bacon!

Since I lost my blue pen I must continue writing with my red pen! Yes my writing must continue! The path is great and the sun was shining. I am finally switching to summer after three the springtime!

Tricastella: I've arrived at the hostel! The path was alright the entire way, even though I got lost and had to follow the road. I was somehow out of it today and just trudged along. I reacquainted with the Franconia man who I first met in Ventosa and then later had as a bed neighbor in Nájera. He is now pain free, which made me so happy because he suffered badly. "The Way gives you that what you need!" I, on the other hand, sat down in a bar, ordered and then drank a bottle of white wine! I rushed through dinner, and I believe I was clearly drunk when I went to bed. It just wasn't a good day for me! It was very interesting how my mood changes with each day!

Daily kms	Total kms
28.1	2285.51

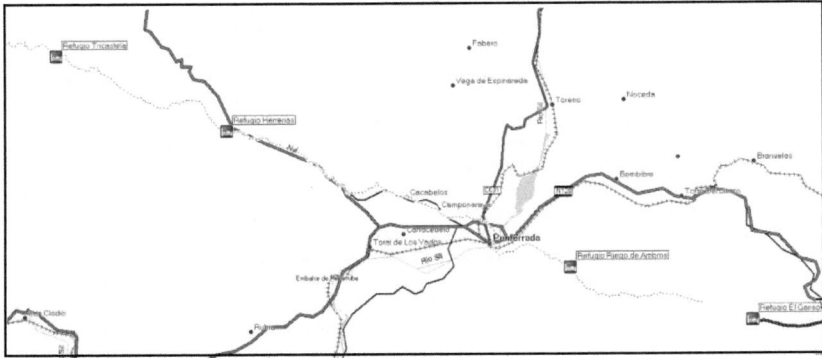

Figure 93: Trail > El Ganso—Triacastella

Day 75, Tricastella to Morgade

First break: Frollais; I finally had breakfast. I haven't decided on my goal yet. Yesterday evening I didn't eat anything, drank too much, and went to bed too late. That was a bad idea, and now I'm not in the best mood! Yikes!

Second break: Sarria; noon; I strolled through an old oak forest that radiated a wonderful ambiance. I sensed something amazing. A particular oak seemed to beckon, compelling me to stand still and place my hands against the tree. Feelings of lightness, understanding, strength and majesty size coursed through me and didn't stop, not even when the past and the future met and said "good day". It was unbelievably moving. I love oaks, it's true! (Author's note: to this day I still understand this experience but it was so great and peaceful and so emotional! Yikes!!!)

Figure 94: Speechless

Third break: Unknown location, but with a bar. After Sarria the route moved steeply uphill through an avenue of oaks. I will try again to give an explanation. They were all ancient oaks! I think they must be over 100 years old. One in particular seemed to call to me. I took off my gloves and touched the tree. I imagined a change in my blood pressure and pulse! I was overflowing with strong emotions, with pleasant feelings of excitement, power, age and future!! At the same time it was a little overwhelming. I started to weep without caring who passed by. I just can't explain it. I felt perfectly at ease, with my spirit and mind balanced. What happened to me?

I've arrived at the hostel: Morgade; it is a private hostel, not too large. Besides, it's less than 100 km from Santiago. After the laundry was hung up, I conversed with a 73 year old lady from Holland in the sun, with a glass of white wine as an aperitif. We then ate dinner with the Alaskan ladies who are also staying here. The conversation was led by the lady from Holland and me. Parallels emerged to Lindsey's former profession. Both cared for kindergarteners.

Daily kms	Total kms
28.4	2313.9

Day 76, Morgade to Palas de Rei

First break: Portomarin; I got breakfast here and then tried to find an internet connection and printer, so I could print out my ticket for my flight home. I did not find one here.

Yesterday I met two German ladies, one of whom had several insect bites. It looked as though she was infected with bedbugs. I gave her my bug spray. She was grateful and I moved on.

Second break: Portos; noon.

Palas de Rei: Today went amazingly well. Santiago seems to be a two day trip away. My mood is slowly sinking because everything is coming to an end! I joined the other pilgrims on the opposite side of the hostel. After the usual round of introductions, I was offered a glass of wine. It went like this: I had to order and pay for a glass of wine at a bar so that I had a glass. When the glass was emptied, it was quickly refilled! Thank goodness I am properly equipped, because without my corkscrew, it would soon be a dry group! When it was my turn to treat, I went into the supermarket, right around the corner and bought a bottle of red wine for 0.99 euros. By dinner time, the entire group was jovial! Then everyone went on their own way to dinner. After dinner I was thoroughly tired and went to bed, but I was no longer alone in my room. A young couple had accommodations at the other end of the room. They had a lot to tell each other during the night, most of it wordless. I felt totally out of place and couldn't even bring myself to go to the bathroom. I longed for the morning so I could finally take off.

Daily kms	Total kms
26.2	2374.03

Figure 95: A jovial circle in Palas de Rei.

Day 77, Palas de Rei to Arzúra

First break: O Coto; breakfast has become yogurt and a banana now. Last night was mentally rough. I became aware that everything will soon be over. It's a shame that my wife was not part of it. Perhaps I will go again with her. Oh, by the way, the fellow wearing the seashell shirt in the picture with me read my mind and booked the last seat on the Ryanair flight from Santiago to Hahn/Germany. He got exactly the day and time he wanted! It was raining but I don't want to take a break. I will continue until I found suitable accommodations!

I arrived in Arzúra but the hostels were full. I chose the first hotel I came to (2 stars). It was nice to have a room to myself again, with the comfort of my own bathroom! I'll finally be able to print out my return ticket, hurray! That was quite an activity! By evening tomorrow I'll be in Santiago! Even there I will go to a boarding house! Once I'm on the way to the End of the World I'll go back to hostels.

Daily kms	Total km
37.6	2411.6

Day 78, Arzúra to Santiago

First break: Calle; breakfast! Still 33 kms to Santiago! I think I'll make it today!

Second break: Amenal; lunch break! Things are going exceptionally well today. I am certain the horse will reach the barn! This is the feeling in me, so I am sure I would enter Santiago!

Third break: Mont Gozo; an incredibly emotional place! I sent Klemens a text to say he knows what I'm seeing! I got his answer, "yes I know". A man from Yugoslavia, accompanied by his wife, addressed me in German so we talked briefly. He is astonished by the distances! At some point the two of them left me. I reach into my backpack and pull out whatever foodstuff is left—a warm can of beer, a mandarin and a banana! I have it all within reach but am incapable of moving. My emotions enveloped me and I cannot control myself. It is at least 15 minutes before my vision clears. The man came around again and apologized that he didn't have a cold beer. Instead he brought me a can of cold coffee! What a sincere gesture. I gave him my thanks! To the right, about 15 meters away, sat a woman of about 30, who took everything in. I don't know why I apologized to her but I did! She says there is a nice hostel up here. But I wanted to reach Santiago today, the path is steeply downhill!

Figure 96: City entrance

At the city entrance; there was still aways to travel to reach the Basilica from the entrance of Santiago de Compostela! I continue on, soon the old city has me in its grasp and the archway is ahead! I walk through the archway and find myself in front of the basilica! I don't know why but I am not very impressed by this place. Why, no high feeling, no satisfied feeling? Why?

Right now it is important for me to find accommodations. I went into an office where I hoped to find out about hotels and guest houses. I stood in line for 30 minutes for nothing. A friendly person told me where I should go. No sooner said than done, I was successful. A guest house in the center of town, not too expensive, it was okay! I got a room and can now concentrate on my Compostella certificate.

It's late afternoon, the line in front of the counter is short, and I now have my Compostela certificate in my hands.

Daily kms	Total kms
37.6	2411.6

I immediately took the certificate back to my room and then went off to shop. Soon I heard a bagpipe in the archway and could not pass it by. I sat down on the steps, listened to the music and drank my can of beer. I was still in my traveling clothes! I love the sound of bagpipes, so I stayed there as long the guy continued playing! After he finished I went to my room cleaned myself up for the evening and dinner.

The evening in Santiago was nice because I was able to do my homework in a street cafe listening to live music! There was a band in the street performing Russian music! Many people passed by; I enjoyed this time immensely. Now I began feeling satisfaction and pride I'd expected. I did it the long way from home to Santiago de Compostela!

I went to bed late.

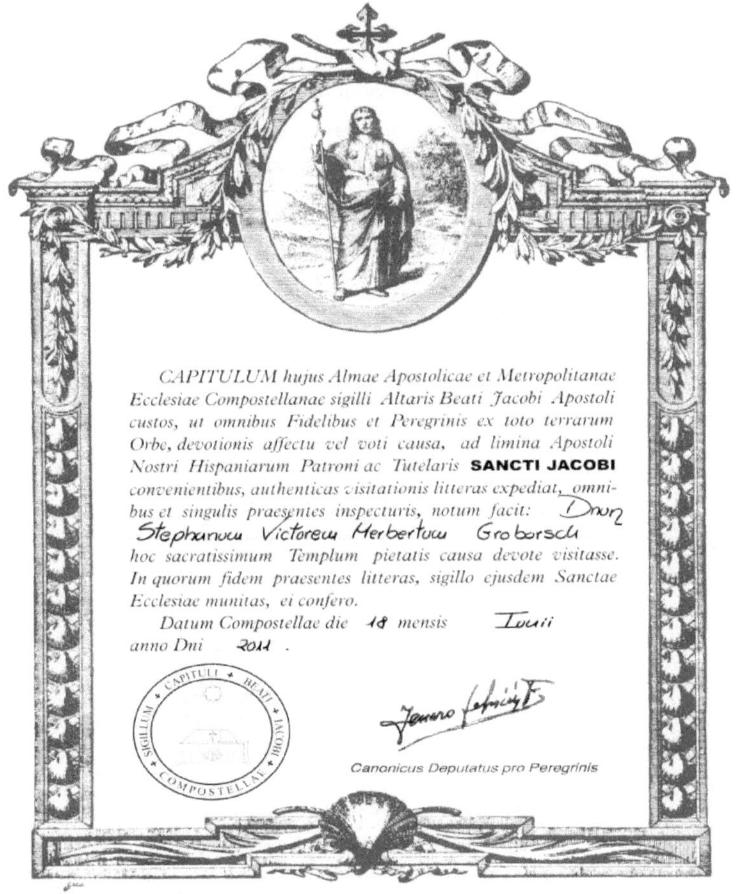

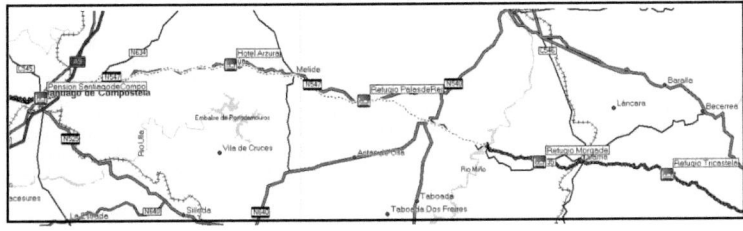

CAPITULUM hujus Almae Apostolicae et Metropolitanae Ecclesiae Compostellanae sigilli Altaris Beati Jacobi Apostoli custos, ut omnibus Fidelibus et Peregrinis ex toto terrarum Orbe, devotionis affectu vel voti causa, ad limina Apostoli Nostri Hispaniarum Patroni ac Tutelaris **SANCTI JACOBI** convenientibus, authenticas visitationis litteras expediat, omnibus et singulis praesentes inspecturis, notum facit: Dnum Stephanum Victorem Herbertum Groborsch hoc sacratissimum Templum pietatis causa devote visitasse. In quorum fidem praesentes litteras, sigillo ejusdem Sanctae Ecclesiae munitas, ei confero.

Datum Compostellae die 18 mensis Iunii anno Dni 2011.

SIGILLUM CAPITULI BEATI JACOBI COMPOSTELLAE

Canonicus Deputatus pro Peregrinis

Figure 97: The certificate

Figure 98: Triacastela to Santiago

Day 79, One Day in Santiago

I woke up late. The day belongs to Santiago and the mass of pilgrims and the vault. I can't say a lot about that. There is a lot of activity in the city. I enjoyed it all and ate well. It was, perhaps, not the most favorable place, but it had great ambience!

Day 80, Santiago to Vilaseno

First break: Ventosa; yesterday was Santiago. Today I'm off to the "End of the World"! The path led uphill through a forest of eucalyptus. Once I reached the top there was a bar offering breakfast. No sooner said than done. Then who should be coming around the corner but the Alaskan ladies. A friendly "hello" and the usual: Where were you? How long have you been in Santiago etc? I continued on my way, who knows when we'll meet again.

Second break: Negreira; I'll be at the hostel in 13 kilometers.

I've arrived at the hostel: Vilaserio; I had a nice dinner, access to a washing machine and dryer, and a good conversation with foreign people, too

Daily kms	Total kms
30.9	2442.51

Day 81, Vilaseno to Oliveiera

Second break: Ponte Oliveiera; the plan to go 40 kilometers to Cée fell through when I received a distress call from the Alaskan ladies. They went about 5-7 kms too far south. I tried to guide them back via texts, but then I walked to meet them. As soon as I made contact with them I was on my way again. It was a bit annoying because it was raining the whole time. After lunch here, I agreed to find accommodations in the next town. We also agreed to meet again for dinner with other pilgrims from all around the world. We ate and talked. It was an enjoyable evening.

Daily kms	Total kms
32.7	2475.29

Day 82, "The End of the World"; Oliveiera to Fisterra

First break: Cée; it was not possible to make it this far yesterday. First because of the weather and second because of the terrain.

On the way up in the hills I saw the Atlantic Ocean for the first time! What a great view! This view motivated me a lot. I think I was on the right path here. It's another 10 km to Fisterra. The late breakfast was good. The ladies always came to breakfast when I had finished eating. This time they asked me to book a place for them in Fisterra. That is not a problem.

I've arrived at the hostel in Fisterra: I was able to pick up the second certificate and prepare myself for the evening. I met the ladies at the entrance to town to show them the way to their certificates and the hostel.

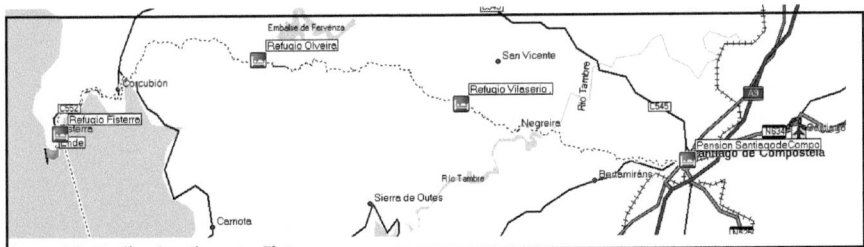

Figure 99: Trail > Santiago to Fisterra

Figure 100: At the entrance to Fisterra, had a quick beer!

Heading to the cape in the evening! But first a final dinner will tke place. We met in a nice restaurant and enjoyed a wonderful dinner. The mood at the table was great, and everyone was looking forward to the next experience.

Cape Finisterre: we started out and arrived as a threesome, after which everyone sought and found their own little corner. One just wants to be alone here at the "End of the World". I met the girls again on the bus to Santiago.

Now I had my time for myself. There is a lot going through my head here— it is really happening! Like the pilgrims before me, I will have to make a decision. What will my next traveling adventure be? Where will I go? Is there another pilgrimage like this one? Will Jerusalem be my goal? Or will I go to Rome? Okay, I have decided the next pilgrimage will be! In 2013 I'm going to Rome! The die is cast! It is funny how I'm reacting in the same way as millions of others before me! But it is how it should be. I just need to figure out how to bring it up to Uschi.

Daily kms	Total kms
36.8	2512.17

Figure 101: The "End of the World"

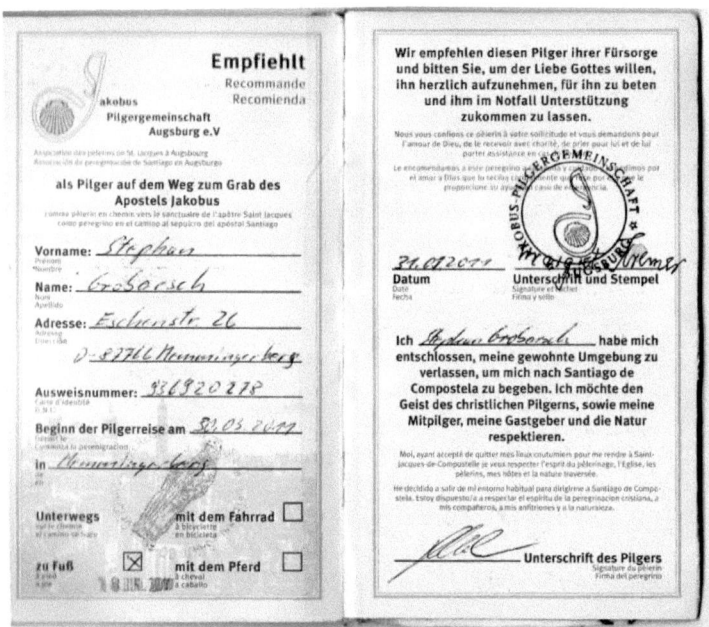

Figure 102: My pilgrim ID

Day 83, Fisterra to Santiago

From now on, everything moved quickly with no detours. Redeployment to Santiago and I bought a ticket to Porto/Portugal. Trying to buy souvenirs in Santiago is still difficult. I decided on "yellow direction arrows" for the adults and a pilgrim figure for the grandchildren. I spent another night in Santiago and enjoyed a good dinner again.

Day 84, Santiago to Porto

When I transferred from Santiago to Porto, there was a great celebration. As I arrived it was St. James Day, which is one of the most important holidays in Portugal. First I settled in and then I walked through the streets of Porto. I was very impressed by the main station. The entrance hall was full of pictures from Portugal's history and all done in tiles. I was there for a long time to take in the pictures! I also found a very fancy cafe and I sat there until the evening came. The streets were full of cheerful people, and in every corner a band was playing. What a massive celebration! The eve of "Fischertag" (a big celebration in Memmingen) doesn't even come close to what is happening here. But it was all a little too much for me. I still felt I wanted to be alone after the pilgrimage…

128

Day 85, Home Again From Porto

I have half a day remaining until my flight home. I visited the city again in the daylight and I was impressed. Porto is a beautiful city.

I got to the airport in the late afternoon and checked in with no problems. I want to get home now so let's take off! I wonder who will be picking me up.

I've landed in Memmingerberg, walked into the concourse and there was the whole gang! My dear wife, hi Uschi, let me embrace you! All the grandchildren with Diana! Siggi with daughter Julia and their child were also there.

Figure 103: Back in Memmingerberg

I'm home!!!!

Texts - St. James correspondence between my brother and me.

Tuesday, 10:47, Stephan

Here my number: 0xxxxxx. Now I also have your No. Greetings, Stephan

Tuesday, 12:55, Klemens

My dear brother, I wish you a good journey as you undertake the risk. Bon chemin, buen camino, good luck, bonne chnce, mucho suerte, lots of luck & God bless!

Thursday, 09:19, Stephan

Good morning, Klemens, Everything's okay here. The night spent in the tent OK. The rain is minor. Greetings, Stephan

Thursday, 09:31, Klemens

Good morning, that's great! Continued good trip! Report again, perhaps with details of next town, then I can be there with you! Regards, Klemens

Thursday, 19:16, Stephan

I was cheeky & procured accommodations. It was more difficult today. I'll take you along with me! Ultreia! (Author's note: "ultreia" is a greeting used between pilgrims on the Camino). Stephan.

Friday, 08:43, Klemens

Thanks for taking me along! You've made good time! Don't overdo it! You can recuperate from tiredness in a day but sprain a muscle or tendon it will take days. Best wishes, Klemens

Friday, 13:22, Stephan

The hostel doesn't answer. Do you have the Augsburg number? Greetings, Stephan shortly before Lindau.

Friday, 13:29, Klemens

Only the number from Mrs. Kremer: 08xxxxx. Lots of luck, Klemens

Friday, 14:57, Klemens

Were you successful? If not, be really brazen & go to rectory, Catholic or Protestant, doesn't matter. Regards Klemens

Friday, 15:43, Stephan

Got him. Clothes are in the washer, I've showered, & am going to chat with Monika Ultreia, Stephan.

Friday, 15:57, Klemens

Super! You're doing great. I wish you good crossing tomorrow & great trip through Switzerland! Ultreia, Klemens

Saturday, 20:11, Stephan

Am in St. Gallen, pilgrim's hostel. Like clockwork Regards, Stephan

Sunday, 15:26, Klemens

Congratulations! It looks as though you're doing everything right. Nevertheless – don't overdo! Good luck, Klemens

Sunday, 19:20, Stephan

I'm camping in Wald! Now I don't know how far I should go tomorrow! Maybe just go by Mt 6:25 - : "Don't worry ...." Regards, Stephen

Sunday, 19:33, Klemens

I suggest lodging in Rapperswil because this side of the river in Zürich is another 1000m elevation to the Etzelpass. You can't do more on that day. Continued good journey! Klemens Klemens

Tuesday, 10:17, Stephan

On my way to Einsiedeln. Took your advice, 15 km bus to Rapperswil. Everything's ok, Regards, Stephan

Tuesday, 11:05, Klemens

Holy cow, boy – give yourself time! In case you get to Einsiedeln & don't find a monastery or hostel, there's a school with rooms & food very reasonable priced. Ultreia Klemens

Tuesday, 19:33, Stephan

Hi, Klemi I'm in Trachselau! I'm not rushing! Took 2 hours for my lunch stew to become edable. The view of the Mythen affected me tremendously! Everything's double green! Regards, Stephan

Tuesday, 19:43, Klemens

You have no idea how much I envy you because you experience everything more intensely then I do on bike. Experience it with every fiber of your being but especially in your soul! Good journey, Klemens

Thursday, 06:44, Klemens

Hello, lonely pilgrim in the Alps, have you conquered Haggenegg? How are you? How's the weather? I wish you joy on the path despite all the efforts! Klemens

Thursday, 09:33, Stephan

Sitting at the Brunnen harbor, waiting to cross to Beckenried. Haggenegg was good & monastery OK. Ultreia, Stephan

Thursday, 19:29, Stephan

Got to Bethanien. Howare things on the home front? Ultreia, Stephan

Thursday 04/07, 20:45, Klemens

No idea where that is. Direction Beckenried? I'm making good progress. Tusday is the last day of rehab. I'll still fearful that you're moving too fast. Take care Klemens

Friday, 18:52, Stephan

Trust! I'm now under Bruningpass! Ultreia, Stephan

Sunday, 19:19, Stephan

I'm in Hiltelfingen at Lake Thun. Still no shipping! Secure lodging again today. Everything ok with you? Ultreia, Stephan

Sunday, 20:47, Klemens

Impressed with your progress! You've got 2 more days to lern French. I'm all right, in rehab till Wednesday, walk without crutches now & then. Good journey! Klemens

Tuesday, 20:20, Stephan

I've taken Fribourg! From the very bottom to the hostel! You'll get home tomorrow! Be happy! Then life without pain can really begin. Ultreia, Stephan

Tuesday, 20:30, Klemens

It just keeps getting better with you! Now it's just a few more days to Genf. No blisters yet? Lost weight? Continued good trip! Klemens

Thursday, 19:47, Stephan

I'm 6.5 km from the Genf Sea, as the crow flies, Had to take a bus for 8 km. Romont, Moudon too near, Lausanne too far! Weight – no idea, no scale! Blister on my right little toe at 11:00 position since Lindau, doesn't bother me. And you? Ultreia, Stephan

Saturday, 16:42, Klemens

I'm happy for you that it's going so well, wishing you many more joy & experiences! Weather seems fine. I'm back jhome, everything's fantastic! Regards, Klemens

Monday, 20:07, Klemens

Well, on your way again? By the way – if you stop off Yenne, Hotel Fer à Cheval gives pilgrims a discount and for a change, a splendid supper! Ultreia, Klemens

Monday, 20:24, Stephan

I'm in Genf! Changed equipment & tomorrow I'll in France! Ultreia, Stephan

Thursday, 10:58, Stephan

Ultreia, Klemi! 15km to Seyssel! Everything's in good shape! That I get to experience this! Regards, Stephan

Friday, 14:01, Klemens

How far did you yesterday? And today's goal? How's the weather? The next few days look the same as at home but with fieldstone churches. Regards, Klemens

Friday, 17:19, Stephan

Hello, Klemi, yesterday as far as Seyssel & today to Lucey Moulin hostel!!! Happy Easter! Stephan

Saturday, 10:17, Klemens

You've a good nose for accommodations! Keep it up! Greetings from Mrs. Kremer & Ultreia! Wishing you a happy Ester & continued good journey, Klemens

Tuesday 04/26, 11:51, Stephan

Hi Klemi set out from Faramans, Assieu seems in range! Everything ok with you? Ultreia, Stephan

Wednesday 04/27, 11:50, Klemens

In that case you'll probably cross the Rhone today. And it begins – until the valley at Lot – the most beautiful stretch of the entire way! Look forward to Le Puy! Ultreia, Klemens

Friday, 13:06, Stephan

10 km to Tence! Everything's ok here: since Fribourg I've stitched my pant 10 times, my shoes are falling apart, looking forward to Le Puy! Perhaps I can find a barbershop on Monday! Ultreia, Stephan

Sunday, 17:13, Stephan

Reached Le Puy & got lodging with friends! Ultreia, Stephan

Sunday, 19:17, Klemens

Congratulations! You've come about 1/3rd of the way. Still enjoying it? You must have breakfast tomorrow, then sing Ultrea and participate in the Pilgrims' Mass at the cathedral! Ultreia, Klemens

Monday, 10:26, Klemens

Well, did you sing Ultreia? Now you're one of millions of pilgrims on the Via Podiensis! Keep your eyes & soul open! Ultreia! Adjuvas Deus te! Klemens

Tuesday 05/03, 12:28, Stephan

Mission accomplished! Many pilgrims have already been this way! Ultreia, Stephan

Thursday, 15:33, Stephan

Greetings from Les Estrets, shortly before Aumont-Aubrac. Laundry day! Ultreia, Stephan

Saturday, 10:49, Klemens

So, well rested & on your way? I really miss that way through Aubrac! Please experience & feel for me also!! Ultreia, Klemens

Sunday, 19:44, Klemens

Hello, Pèlerin St. Jacques, I dont know where you are right now but `try to get to the Pilgrims' mass in Conques at 7 or 8 am. Klemens

Sunday, 21:18, Stephan

I'm in Estaing now! Ultreia-"Ever onward", Stephan

Friday, 18:37, Stephan

Hello, Klemi! I'm with the nuns in Vaylats. Tomorrow I'll be southward towards Toulouse. I'm look forward to Lourdes. Nice weather! Ultreia, Stephan

Friday, 23:00, Klemens

Greetings to the daughters of Jesus! Already turning south? You'll miss Cahors with the Valentré bridge! Why not go to Lectoure & pick up GR65 (yellow/red) toward Auch (sister city of Memmingen) & then on to Lourdes & Somport! You'll find more reasonabley priced gîtes there! As always, happy trails! Perserve! Klemens

Thursday, 09:33, Klemens

Everything ok with you? Is Lourdes already on the horizon? I wish you a nice stay & then a good trip to Somport! Don't give up! Klemens

Thursday, 11:51, Stephan

Another hour to Lourdes. I'm in Bartrès. Tomorrow will be a day of rest, writing mail & buying a train ticket to Somport. Once there, You'll be with me again! Ultreia, Stephan

Friday, 13:54, Stephan

Greetings from your former comrades from FFB airfield!

Friday, 13:57, Klemens

1. Congratulations on your arrival in Lourdes! 2. I'd like to know more detail. 3. Greetings to you too, Ultreia, Clement

Friday 05/20, 14:02, Stephan

Karin with husband & Pottinger with wife

Friday, 15:37, Stephan

Shell I send greetings from you?

Saturday, 17:46, Stephan

Somport is behind me! Jaca 15 km in front of me! You're with me again! Ultreia, Stephan

Sunday, 19:55, Klemens

Greetings from wife & yours & all folks in Kaufbeuren. Under no circumstances should you miss Eunate (about 5 days away)!

Wednesday, 15:59, Stephan

I've reached Monreal! I'll try to stay overnight in Eunate! Ultreia, Stephan

Thursday, 17:19, Klemens

In the southwest you should see the gem of Navarre Romanesque period. The little house next door takes pilgrims. Otherwise 5 km to Obanos.

Thursday, 17:27, Stephan

I spent an hour in Eunate, it was great!!! I'm past the bridge, first hostel. Ultreia, Stephan

Sunday, 19:15, Stephan

I hope you all had a nice weekend. Am now in Nájera. Everything's okay! Ultreia, Stephan

Sunday 05/29th, 19:54, Klemens

You're doing really well! And how did you feel for 60 days & over 2000 km over Puente la Reina like millons before you?! (meself also!) It's wonderful for me to be able to experience each km again with you. Thank you!!! At Santo Doming de la Calzada you will really be going through the Meseta. I wish you perseverance & enlightening experiences! Klemens

Wednesday, 19:17, Stephan

Burgos! I don't know yet how far I'll go tomorrow. Hostel vacancies are scarce! Ultreia, Stephan

Wednesday, 10:13, Stephan

I'm drinking coffee in Leòn! All the best! Ultreia, Stephan

Sunday, 17:44, Klemens

Hello little brother on the Camino, everything ok with you? Another 2 hills as well as 2 high points (Cruz de Ferro & O`Cebreiro), then sadly, the end is soon. Klemens

Sunday, 17:56, Stephan

Cruz was yesterday & very emotional! Ultreia

Sunday, 18:47, Klemens

Congratulations! And O`Cebreiro will be that way as well!!! Ultreia! Ever onward, ever higher! I'llbe with you! Greetings from the van Gogh on the Rhône.

Wednesday, 15:57, Klemens

Hello Stephen, greetings from Karin & me on the Rhône! In an hour we'll be crossing the bridge at Chavanay = St James Way! Good trek & Ultreia, Clement

Wednesday, 16:21, Stephan

It's almost done! Less than 100 km! I'll still go to the Cape. Enjoy the river! Ultreia!

Friday, 22:06, Klemens

I wish you all the best for for advocacy in Santiago on the last bit of your trip as pilgrim. Ultreia & bon voyage! Let us know when you're in Monte Gozo! Klemens

Saturday, 16:18, Stephan

Hi, Brother, you know what we're looking at! - Greet Karin, Ultreia, Stephan

Saturday, 16:26, Klemens

Thank you that you take me with you! I'm excited again. Please hug for me! Kick up your heels a pilgrimage fair! I'm glad for you! Ultreia, Klemens

Saturday, 18:47, Stephan

Mission accomplished! Monday it goes to the Cape! Of emotions! Regards, Stephan

Monday, 12:50, Stephan

Santiago is history! Ultreia Fisterre! Regards, Stephan

Tuesday, 12:33, Klemens

You are well advised to go to the Cape at the "End of the World", even if you seem to over 3000 km on the reef on the sea for no reason again "losgeheult" (start to cry). Ultreia, Klemens

Friday 06/24, 17:21, Klemens

Hello brother, I wish you a safe journey home, come home safe! Regards, Clemens

Sunday 06/26, 09:36, Klemens

Where in the world you put? Do I have to come looking for you? Klemens

(After that phone call from Stephen, a little longer, emotional conversation)

The Way in Numbers

Date	Daily km	Hours in Travel	Average Speed	Elevation in Meters (ASL)	GPS in process	Total km	Time
03.30.11	10,2	02:04	4,9	596	02:51	10,17	10:12
	21,8	04:23	5	676	05:55	21,82	13:16
	26,8	05:23	5	692	08:51	26,76	16:12
	31,3	06:16	5	663	10:16	31,28	17:37
	33,9	06:50	5	697	11:05	33,93	18:26
03.31.11	5,29	01:10	4,5	671	01:38	39,38	9:05
	8,89	01:59	4,5	679	03:15	43,07	10:41
	13,4	02:59	4,5	681	04:42	47,51	12:08
	20,9	04:34	4,6	573	07:57	55,03	15:24
04.01.11	6,42	01:10	4,8	554	01:44	61,7	10:12
	13,8	02:54	4,8	540	03:45	69,12	12:13
	20,4	04:11	4,9	437	06:49	75,65	15:15
04.02.11	3,28	00:37	5,2	411	01:21	78,93	11:25
	25,3	02:38	9,6	588	05:36	100,98	15:39
	28,4	03:18	8,6	577	06:37	104,06	16:40
	35,7	04:28	8	682	08:42	111,31	18:57
04.03.11	5,43	01:01	5,3	637	01:47	116,93	10:09
	9,29	02:00	4,6	834	03:57	120,79	12:20
	12,3	02:49	4,9	991	06:35	123,82	14:57
	13,7	03:08	4,4	1016	07:37	125,19	15:55
	16,7	03:45	4,4	844	08:24	128,19	16:46

Date	Daily km	Hours in Travel	Average Speed	Elevation in Meters (ASL)	GPS in process	Total km	Time
04.04.11	4,71	00:59	4,8	691	01:11	132,99	8:52
	9,81	02:06	4,6	8,28	02:55	138,12	10:35
	14	02:55	4,8	609	04:02	142,33	11:42
	19,3	03:48	5	00:00	05:43	147,54	13:24
	23,6	04:55	4,8	787	07:47	151,86	15:28
	26,2	05:29	4,8	736	08:43	154,53	16:24
04.05.11	5,01	01:05	4,6	586	02:17	179,03	10:01
	7,35	01:42	4,3	862	04:34	181,38	12:18
	12,5	02:58	4,2	928	07:49	186,49	15:33
	17,2	03:56	4,4	417	09:22	191,24	17:17
04.06.11	6,07	01:10	4,5	1404	03:06	197,8	11:04
	7,95	01:46	4,5	897	04:32	199,69	12:30
	15,9	06:23	4,7	896	08:11	207,63	16:30
04.07.11	12,9	:48	16,1	440	01:24	220,54	10:31
	20,8	02:38	7,9	521	03:43	228,46	12:50
	28,3	04:19	6,6	586	06:46	235,97	15:54
	32,1	05:09	6,2	694	08:18	239,68	17:26
	34,6	05:46	6	797	09:20	242,25	18:25
04.08.11	7,57	01:34	4,8	501	02:45	249,82	11:47
	9,88	02:02	4,8	534	03:33	252,19	13:09
	17,1	03:33	4,8	671	06:22	259,36	16:00
04.09.11	2,32	:28	4,9	1048	02:12	216,69	9:30
	5,29	01:07	4,7	691	04:14	264,67	11:35
	12,9	02:41	4,8	611	06:37	272,26	16:13
	15,6	03:13	4,8	628	07:38	274,99	17:15

Date	Daily km	Hours in Travel	Average Speed	Elevation in Meters (ASL)	GPS in process	Total km	Time
04.10.11	4,65	:54	5,1	435	01:30	279,72	8:58
	10,1	01:58	5,1	748	03:31	285,29	11:22
	14	02:40	5,3	546	04:59	289,12	12:59
	17,5		5	611	06:45	292,55	15:59
	21,6	04:26	4,9	570	08:28	296,72	18:00
04.11.11	9,13	01:36	5,7	585	02:19	305,84	10:56
	14,3	02:40	5,3	719	04:13	311,04	13:02
	19,4	03:40	5,3	778	06:16	316,17	16:10
04.12.11	7,45	01:42	4,4	804	02:13	330,74	11:15
	18,1	04:00	4,5	645	06:00	08:52	15:29
	23,4	05:11	4,5	640	08:06	346,71	17:45
04.13.11	5,68	01:15	4,5	681	02:28	352,39	10:30
	13,4	02:57	4,6	646	04:59	360,14	13:17
	19,9	04:25	4,5	685	06:50	366,58	15:58
	22,3	04:57	4,5	768	07:55	368,97	17:00
04.14.11	10,5	02:17	4,6	503	02:59	379,44	11:18
	14,7	03:09	4,7	529	04:20	383,69	13:00
	21,7	04:42	4,6	759	06:34	390,68	16:17
	24,4	05:17	4,6	747	07:31	393,37	17:16
	34	05:40	6	876	08:27	402,99	18:44
04.15.11	9,1	01:41	5,4	383	02:40	412,19	10:16
	13,7	02:40	5,1	386	04:32	416,8	13:04
	24,1	04:44	5,1	389	08:05	427,15	16:40
	33,9	04:56	6,9	418	08:47	437,04	17:15
04.16.11	10,9	02:10	5	425	02:55	447,95	11:40
	13,9	02:48	4,9	409	04:12	461,83	11:52

Date	Daily km	Hours in Travel	Average Speed	Elevation in Meters (ASL)	GPS in process	Total km	Time
04.17.11	6,43	01:17	5	416	01:56	454,38	9:37
	15,8	03:13	4,9	434	05:11	463,79	13:04
04.18.11	5,51	01:49		379	01:49	469,3	10:45
	9,16	01:50	5	371	03:20	472,95	12:57
	15,2	02:30	6,1	410	04:35	479,01	14:54
04.19.11	7,17	01:17	5,5	430	02:02	486,21	10:43
	14,4	02:50	5,1	527	04:01	493,47	12:50
	17,5	03:32	4,9	745	05:51	496,51	15:00
04.20.11	5,1	01:08	4,5	896	02:37	501,72	10:09
	13	02:51	4,6	727	05:03	509,58	13:14
	22	04:49	4,6	612	08:28	518,6	17:30
04.21.11	4,4	:50	5,2	330	01:11	523,01	9:10
	8,19	01:45	4,7	488	02:42	526,81	10:45
	16,7	03:34	4,7	269	05:40	535,37	13:41
04.22.11	9,25	01:49	5,1	250	02:19	544,62	10:18
	20,4	04:06	5	244	05:44	555,73	14:40
	26,2	05:22	4,9	358	08:06	561,61	17:04
04.23.11	11,5	02:22	4,8	239	03:20	573,24	11:21
	16,5	03:29	4,7	620	05:21	578,07	13:58
	23,4	04:56	4,7	652	07:35	585,05	17:15
04.24.11	7,48	01:31	4,9	243	02:07	592,55	10:30
	12,8	02:40	4,8	330	03:38	597,84	11:57
	19,9	04:14	4,7	412	05:51	605	14:10
	24	05:11	4,6	518	07:33	609,11	16:27
	33,8	07:09	4,7	532	10:18	618,83	19:12
	18,3	03:46	4,8	451	05:00	637,19	14:10

Date	Daily km	Hours in Travel	Average Speed	Elevation in Meters (ASL)	GPS in process	Total km	Time
04.25.11	10,1	02:07	4,8	491	02:56	629,05	11:35
	23,4	04:50	4,8	394	06:22	642,29	15:48
	33,1	06:51	4,8	378	09:09	652	18:35
04.26.11	12,3	02:36	4,7	406	03:08	664,26	11:15
	19,4	04:13	4,6	448	05:13	671,42	14:02
	39	08:33	4,6	188	10:49	690,99	20:03
04.27.11	5,67	01:18	4,3	246	02:04	696,66	10:10
	10,8	02:37	4,1	394	03:54	701,81	12:13
	18,5	04:24	4,2	692	06:30	709,46	15:33
	22,1	05:17	4,2	602	07:57	713,11	17:00
04.28.11	6,3	01:27	4,3	547	01:57	719,14	10:14
	17,8	03:55	4,5	1151	07:02	730,89	15:35
	23	04:41	4,9	828	06:58	754,02	16:46
04.30.11	12,9	02:46	4,6	1039	04:01	767,11	11:15
	19	04:10	4,6	1187	06:13	773,2	15:01
05.01.11	16,1	03:14	5	677	03:52	789,31	12:02
	25,1	05:00	4,9	621	06:10	798,28	15:02
	27	527	4,9	672	06:53	800,24	15:30
05.02.11	Le Puy a day of rest						
05.03.11	16,6	03:18	5	1117	03:51	817,58	11:48
	23,2	04:33	5,1	881	05:33	824,12	14:20
	29,8	05:49	5,1	614	07:32	830,69	16:21
05.04.11	11,4	02:15	5	959	03:02	842,19	10:43
	21	04:08	5,1	1148	05:23	851,79	13:44
	29,2	05:51	5	1299	08:14	860,39	16:40
	35,3	06:55	5,1	1178	09:55	866,13	18:20

Date	Daily km	Hours in Travel	Average Speed	Elevation in Meters (ASL)	GPS in process	Total km	Time
05.05.11	8,09	01:36	5	987	02:16	874,23	10:00
	15,4	03:08	4,9	931	04:53	881,54	13:45
05.06.11	8,36	01:37	5,1	1062	02:04	889,93	10:01
	16,3	03:10	5,1	1120	03:50	897,86	11:59
	24,3	04:49	5	1197	05:42	905,87	14:33
05.07.11	8,15	01:34	5,2	1182	01:41	914,07	9:42
	16,5	03:19	5	1309	03:50	922,46	12:34
05.08.11	11,6	02:16	5,1	397	03:08	940,83	11:04
	15,3	03:03	5	350	04:41	944,64	13:29
	25,1	04:57	5,1	335	07:11	954,39	16:23
05.09.11	10,6	02:05	5,1	646	03:18	968,33	11:35
	19	03:42	5,1	402	05:14	976,7	14:09
	21,8	04:19	5	511	06:03	979,49	15:54
05.10.11	14,4	02:51	5	534	04:02	993,91	11:26
05.11.11	18,4	03:42	5	289	04:34	1024,4	12:19
	26,5	05:18	5	214	06:36	1032,43	14:57
	32,6	06:30	5	306	08:51	1038,6	17:41
05.12.11	14,6	02:52	5,1	378	03:14	1053,21	10:50
	24,9	04:49	5,2	163	05:38	1063,55	13:33
	29,3	05:43	5,1	184	06:50	1067,94	15:26
05.13.11	13,4	02:40	5	306	03:16	1081,44	10:24
	20,8	04:06	5	332	05:09	1088,77	12:50
	29,1	05:45	5,1	304	07:20	1097,07	15:24
05.14.11	26,4	04:51	5,4	133	05:21	1123,68	13:28
05.15.11	18,4	03:30	5,2	88	03:54	1142,06	12:18
	26,7	05:03	5,3	99	05:44	1150,37	14:27

Date	Daily km	Hours in Travel	Average Speed	Elevation in Meters (ASL)	GPS in process	Total km	Time
05.16.11	10,02	01:55	5,3	97	02:13	1160,79	10:42
	24,5	04:35	5,3	126	05:05	1175,09	13:59
	27,6	05:15	5,2	161	06:03	1178,19	15:00
	65,1	06:51	10,4	169	07:39	1215,7	16:50
05.17.11	65,7	00:36	109	291	00:46	1281,44	9:55
	71	01:37	43,9	274	01:57	1286,66	11:20
	78	02:53	27	328	03:22	1293,69	
	86,2	04:19	19,2	379	05:08	1301,94	15:34
	92,6	05:38	16,4	418	06:51	1308,35	17:28
05.18.11	1,05		5				7:30
	49,7	47	63,1	258	01:05	1358,02	8:17
	52,3	01:18	40	265	01:45	1360,64	8:57
	59,1	02:38	22,4	276	03:13	1367,41	10:32
	68	04:19	15,7	330	05:10	1376,33	13:11
	75,8	05:38	13,4	330	06:59	1384,09	15:28
05.19.11	18	03:27	5,2	505	04:20	1402,09	11:32
20.05.201	Lourdes a day of rest						
05.21.11	1,98	:20	5,8	407	:29	1410,48	7:23
	41,2	:48	51,1	199	01:05	1449,71	8:13
	76,5	01:25	53,5	228	01:56	1485,06	9:53
	132	02:39	49,8	1611	03:20	1540,42	11:33
	139	03:57	35	1291	05:05	1547,08	13:28
	164	05:40	28,8	1069	07:25	1572,01	16:06
05.22.11	14,3	02:47	5,1	830	03:09	1586,35	10:32
	25,5	04:49	5,1	680	05:45	1597,52	14:23
	28,9	05:43	5,1	651	06:41	1601,07	15:40

Date	Daily km	Hours in Travel	Average Speed	Elevation in Meters (ASL)	GPS in process	Total km	Time
05.23.11	6,49	01:16	5,1	599	01:35	1607,72	8:22
	17,1	03:18	5,2	596	03:49	1618,34	10:57
	40,8	03:18	5,6	560	08:15	1642,02	15:52
05.24.11	10,4	01:59	5,2	638	02:20	1653,04	10:58
	21,3	04:04	5,2	406	04:39	1663,88	14:10
05.25.11	8,57	01:53	4,6	720	02:15	1672,55	8:55
	17,5	03:44	4,7	721	04:33	1681,42	11:15
	27,4	05:42	4,8	556	06:53	1691,33	14:12
05.26.11	12,4	02:34	4,8	586	03:22	1703,83	9:54
	25,4	05:00	5,1	397	06:00	1716,85	12:52
	32,3	06:41	5,2	388	07:28	1723,69	14:49
05.27.11	21,6	04:06	5,3	434	04:37	1745,35	11:21
	42,8	08:01	5,3	461	09:11	1766,51	17:23
05.28.11	17,9	03:35	5	471	04:00	1784,4	11:02
	27,4	05:31	5	408	06:09	1793,98	14:00
05.29.11	11,9	02:24	4,9	507	02:53	1805,87	9:00
	18,6	03:49	4,9	641	04:58	1812,61	11:19
	29,7	05:59	5	499	07:43	1823,68	14:22
	14,3	03:05	4,6	716	03:25	1837,94	10:04
	22,2	04:36	4,8	574	05:18	1845,87	12:30
	29,3	06:13	4,7	741	07:13	1853,01	15:00
05.31.11	5,56	01:13	4,6	764	01:26	1858,84	8:52
	15,4	03:06	5	797	03:31	1868,73	11:13
	26,4	04:56	5,3	896	05:31	1879,68	13:54
	30,2	05:44	5,3	948	06:31	1883,46	15:30
06.01.11	10,9	02:13	4,9	1004	02:57	1894,35	9:55

Date	Daily km	Hours in Travel	Average Speed	Elevation in Meters (ASL)	GPS in process	Total km	Time
	29,7	06:13	4,8	990	07:25	1913,17	14:59
	36,9	07:34	4,9	912	09:26	1920,4	17:11
06.02.11	12,4	02:35	4,8	829	03:05	1932,86	9:31
	20,5	04:02	4,7	829	05:00	1940,93	11:55
06.03.11	13,9	02:30	5,5	869	02:41	1954,84	8:52
	23	04:15	5,4	824	04:53	1963,9	11:30
	34,2	06:35	5,2	781	07:42	1375,11	15:04
06.04.11	13,9	03:01	4,6	790	03:20	1989,05	9:55
	28,2	05:48	4,9	810	06:16	2003,29	13:27
	33,7	06:54	4,9	847	07:38	2008,84	14:58
06.05.11	27,2	05:15	5,2	888	5,58	2036,33	13:28
06.06.11	13,9	02:30	5,3	852	02:38	2049,47	8:50
	23,3	04:27	5,2	863	04:48	2059,64	11:52
	31,2	06:02	5,2	885	06:36	2067,49	14:35
06.07.11	12,9	02:26	5,3	832	02:39	2080,44	9:18
	19,4	03:37	5,4	808	04:06	2086,96	11:12
06.08.11	12,7	02:20	5,4	849	02:47	2105,92	10:01
	19,1	03:29	5,5	918	04:31	2112,36	12:00
	29,3	05:33	5,3	886	06:52	2122,56	14:56
	33,6	06:21	5,3	889	07:59	2166,85	16:00
	14,7	02:46	5,3	838	03:05	2141,55	10:29
	20,2	03:46	5,3	859	04:13	2147,05	12:08
06.10.11	12	02:29	4,8	877	02:51	2159,09	9:32
	21,1	04:21	4,8	984	04:58	2168,16	12:06
	25,3	05:14	4,8	1000	05:57	2172,36	13:07
06.11.11	7,35	01:21	5,4	1152	01:30	2179,91	8:28

Date	Daily km	Hours in Travel	Average Speed	Elevation in Meters (ASL)	GPS in process	Total km	Time
	24	04:40	5,1	1163	05:16	2196,58	13:40
06.12.11	4,83	:57	3	990	01:06	2205,52	8:16
	16,3	03:06	5,2	537	03:38	2216,98	11:50
	20,8	03:54	5,3	505	05:05	2212,45	13:42
	27,4	05:04	5,4	475	06:47	2228,08	15:30
06.13.11	8,58	01:35	5,4	517	01:49	2236,66	8:37
	17,8	03:10	5,6	590	03:50	2245,88	
	29,3	05:17	5,5	709	06:34	2257,37	15:00
06.14.11	6,96	01:33	4,5	1308	02:06	2264,33	8:39
	18,9	03:42	5,1	1300	04:26	2276,23	11:30
	28,1	05:22	5,2	674	06:17	2285,51	15:00
06.15.11	8,48	01:33	5,2	667	02:17	2294	9:00
	16,1	03:02	5,3	479	03:55	2301,61	11:00
	24,4	05:39	5,2	621	05:53	2309,88	13:33
	28,4	05:25	5,2	653	06:51	2913,96	15:00
06.16.11	9,82	01:53	5,2	379	02:13	2323,72	8:54
	16,8	03:12	5,3	567	03:54	2330,74	10:59
	28,3	05:15	5,3	585	06:10	2342,25	13:59
	33,9	06:20	5,3	601	0,423	2347,86	16:30
06.17.11	7,71	01:30	5,1	483	01:58	2355,57	8:46
	20,9	03:55	5,3	416	04:46	2368,74	11:49
	26,2	04:55	5,3	401	06:10	2374,03	14:00
	21,3	03:51	5,5	261	04:58	2395,31	12:23
	37,6	06:43	5,6	260	08:49	2411,6	17:00
06.19.11	Santiago enjoy the day						
06.20.11	8,19	01:34	5,2	180	02:08	2419,83	9:15

Date	Daily km	Hours in Travel	Average Speed	Elevation in Meters (ASL)	GPS in process	Total km	Time
	19,5	03:39	5,3	175	04:42	2431,16	12:16
	30,9	05:49	5,3	344	07:35	2442,51	16:27
06.21.11	30,6	05:34	5,5	269	06:08	2473,2	13:33
	32,7	05:58	5,5	281	06:50	2475,29	15:28
06.22.11	20,8	03:50	5,4	11	04:21	2469,15	11:27
	34,1	06:11	5,5	26	07:15	2509,45	15:30
06.23.11	from Finesterre to Santiago						
06.24.11	Santiago to Porto						
06.25.11	Porto flying to MM airport 21:00 lcl landing time